ANSWERS TO PRAISE

MERLIN R. CAROTHERS

ANSWERS TO PRAISE

MERLIN R. CAROTHERS

Logos International
Plainfield, New Jersey

All Scriptures are from the King James Version of the Bible unless otherwise indicated. Scriptures marked TLB are taken from *The Living Bible: Paraphrased* (Wheaton, Ill.: Tyndale House Publishers, © 1971), and are used by permission.

ANSWERS TO PRAISE
Copyright © 1972 by Logos International
All rights reserved
Printed in the United States of America
International Standard Book Number: 0-88270-015-4
Library of Congress Card Number: 72-86262
Published by Logos International, Plainfield, New Jersey

Other books by Merlin Carothers:

Prison to Praise

Power in Praise

PUBLISHER'S NOTE

There is a story behind the genesis of this book that is simply too good not to tell. It says something about Merlin Carothers' writing, something about the way Logos operates, and a great deal about Who's in charge in both situations.

It begins some months ago. Though *Prison to Praise* had yet to appear on any bestseller lists, its popularity was certainly obvious to the boys in the shipping room, who were shipping thousands every week.

I called Merlin to get him moving on the sequel, and to see if he had a title yet. He didn't. But as we discussed it, he happened to mention that he was already getting some wonderful letters in response to the first book and perhaps they could be worked into the sequel, which was shaping up to be an extension of the first, with more teaching.

"*Answers to Praise*—that's what we'll call it," I heard myself say, and already I could envision the ad layout, the jacket copy, and the line on the order form. From vision to fact seems to occur with lightning swiftness around here, and before a month went by, *Answers to Praise* was being advertised in the back of Logos paperbacks and on our order forms as Merlin's next book.

But in the Kingdom, things don't always go according to man's plan. Merlin was led to leave the letters out of the second book, which concentrated on the teaching of his old, yet remarkably new, message: that we are indeed to praise God in all circumstances. And the Lord gave the title: *Power in Praise*—strong, bold, and dramatic, the perfect touchstone to the content and tenor of the book.

So, we had to notify all our bookstore accounts, change the order forms, and inform those who had already placed orders, that the working title, *Answers to*

Praise, had been changed to *Power in Praise*. And that should have taken care of it.

But it didn't. Orders kept coming in for *Answers to Praise,* with notes like, "Thank you very much for the fifty copies of *Power in Praise.* I'm sure we will do quite well with them. But please send fifty *Answers to Praise,* which is what we ordered in the first place."

Finally the situation was desperately critical. I got on the phone to Merlin. "Listen. You've got to write a book called *Answers to Praise.* We've gotten thousands of advance orders for a book that doesn't exist, and we try to tell them that there is no such book, but they won't believe us. And some of them even refuse to take their advance payments back!"

Merlin was nonplussed. "Well," he finally said, "I'm getting some great letters about *Power in Praise*, too —"

"We'll do what we did with Nicky Cruz in *The Lonely Now*, publish the best of the letters with your replies, and let the Holy Spirit do the selecting and the editing."

And that is exactly what happened. Almost in less time than it takes to tell about it. Praise the Lord that He is in control of the situation, because we certainly aren't!

Dan Malachuk

FOREWORD

A Week in Ambia

Life as a Methodist pastor can be very exciting. As I write this here in Ambia, Indiana, I'm reflecting over this past week. As usual it has been crammed full of continual activity.

A man drove from Michigan to request prayer for healing and to be filled with the Holy Spirit. He is an executive for a successful company and attends a Pentecostal-type church. He knew the right terminology, but was filled with fears, driven by bad habits, physically a wreck from guilt, and hungering for more of God "if it could be found." By the time he left, he was laughing and crying at the same time. He said a great burden had left his heart; he spoke in a new language, and was thoroughly baptized in the Holy Spirit.

Another day a man arrived here from Los Angeles, California. He was desperate. After reading *Prison to Praise* he was determined to come and be prayed for. I usually discourage long trips, but this man didn't even call to see if I would be at home. He said, "I was so desperate I would have kept coming back until you were at home!"

I told him that Jesus was his answer, and that he could have been healed and baptized wherever he was. As I ministered to him, joy replaced the days of desperation. As we prayed, Jesus flooded his heart, and he was healed in body and spirit. He floated out the door, nearly unaware of my presence, but with a new knowledge that Jesus is alive!

A man who ministers as a layman with the Methodist Lay Witness movement came by on his way to another state. We had prayer, and he decided to stay with us for a prayer group we were having in our home that evening. He was a blessing to us, and he said we blessed him. At this prayer group, the second one in our home here in Ambia, twenty-one people attended, and God poured out blessings. Three college boys came, and Jesus baptized them in His Spirit. By the time they left, they were so filled with joy they were actually "unspeakable."

The week was going beautifully, and a new piece of news made it even better! My wife Mary and I are scheduled to go to California for five days of meetings at the end of this month. We received a letter this week from Pat Boone inviting us to come and visit Shirley and him while we are there. This was significant to me, as I received two letters this week from people to whom Pat had given copies of *Prison to Praise.*

So many beautiful things have happened this week that remind me of how God has blessed so continuously over the past few years. A new door opened this week and I do not know where it may lead. A member of my church approached me about the possibility of starting a radio program that he would get other men to sponsor. I went with him to a radio station to discuss the possibilities. Everything looks as if it will develop. As we expected, we learned there are no religious radio programs being broadcast in this entire area, and one is positively needed. These are not wealthy men sponsoring this idea, but men with a vision to do something for Christ.

Throughout the week, many other things have happened, but these are a few that cling to my mind as reasons for being glad to be alive and glad to be serving Him! Right beside me, Mary has been enjoying equal blessings from God. She started a weekly ladies' Bible-study class here in our home, and over thirty women attended. Many of them said they had never enjoyed studying the Bible before as they did in this class! What a blessed week this has been! And what blessed years these are as we praise Him for all that is.

Answers to Praise has been compiled from actual case histories of other people who are learning the power in praise. It is my prayer that these testimonies will set you to praising, that you may know His abundant life alive in you.

TERMITES

Dear Rev. Carothers,

After I read your books, the first irritation I thought of was the termites in our house. They were literally eating us out of house and home. Every day I had to sweep all over the house to clean up the sawdust from their continued devouring of our wooden structure. Six months ago, I had started to pray that God would stop these little monsters. Over and over, I claimed the house for God and tried to believe He would stop them. Exterminators tried every trick of the trade. Nothing helped. When I finished your first book, I decided to thank God for the termites. All over the house, I looked at their leavings and thanked the Lord that they were supplying exactly what I needed. My private war was over, and I was at peace.

The next morning, I dreaded to go through the house, but I again determined to thank the Lord for every evidence of the termites' efforts to eat our house out from under us. But I couldn't do it! I couldn't find any evidence of their work. The next day I was even more surprised—no evidence again! It has been several months now, and no sign of termites.

I wouldn't have believed it if anyone had told me the story, but I know you will. I'm really quite a sane, ordinary housewife, but God has used this simple lesson to teach me something very wonderful. I'm thanking God for everything now, and other "termites" are fading out of my life.

My Comments

Little worms eat away at the insides of many people. Be they ever so small, they gradually destroy peace of mind. You do not have to put up with their persistent efforts to eat you out of the kingdom of peace Jesus wants to build within you.

"Peace be within thy walls, and prosperity within thy palaces" (Ps. 122:7).

FOUR-YEAR-OLD PRAYS FOR MOTHER'S HEALING

Dear Rev. Carothers,

When I learned I was expecting my fourth child, I was exasperated. Many years had passed since the birth of our third child. I was unusually old, in my opinion, to be expecting again, and resented this unexpected intrusion in my life. The baby was born with no complications—mother and child were healthy. I heard you speaking on praising the Lord for everything and committed myself to praising God continually. With a rather weak faith, but a strong determination, I praised the Lord for our new child.

However, a few months later I gradually became aware that something very serious was happening to my arms. An examination revealed wheatlike cancer growths in the muscles. In a series of operations, doctors cut away parts of my arm muscles. By the time our baby was four years old, I had completely lost the use of my arms and was unable to fulfill any duties as a wife and mother. Friends and relatives came in daily to do even the most simple tasks, and my life became filled with grief that I was so completely helpless. Over and over, I begged God to heal me, but my faith was unable to believe His promises. Several prayer groups prayed regularly for me, but their prayers did not seem to be answered.

One morning our four-year-old baby girl said to me, "Mommy, can I pray for Jesus to heal your arms?"

2

To humor the child, I somewhat absentmindedly said, "Why, sure, you can pray for me."

The child took hold of my limp hands and prayed a simple prayer. When my husband came home for lunch, our little girl was in the kitchen playing. He said to her, "Was your aunt here this morning?"

"No."

"Was Grandmother here?"

"No."

"Who set the table for dinner?"

"Mommy did."

"How could Mommy do that, dear? She isn't able."

"Oh, Jesus healed her this morning."

My husband ran to find me, and I greeted him with my arms lifted high over my head.

"Yes, Jesus healed me! My arms are well!"

I praised God for a nearly unwanted baby, and He used her to heal me. If He had not given me this child, I might never have been healed. When I went back to the doctor for an examination, they could find absolutely no trace of cancer, and now months later, my arms are growing stronger every day.

My Comments

There is so very much that we do not know about receiving God's healing power. Remember that in this case God started a plan nearly five years prior to the actual healing and then used the simple faith of a little girl. His procedures may tend to frustrate us, but remember that He is God and that He loves us with perfect love. He wants such trust from us as He received from Paul in prison after he had been beaten and chained in an underground cell.

"At midnight Paul and Silas prayed, and sang praises unto God: and the prisoners heard them" (Acts 16:25).

PROFESSOR'S DAUGHTER IN JUVENILE HOME

Dear Mr. Carothers,

I am a professor in a distinguished and well-known college. My wife and I have been Christians most of our lives. When our sixteen-year-old daughter had a severe problem, we were in total confusion as to what we should do. She had become involved with a married man. When the problem was discovered, our daughter insisted she loved the man and would continue to be with him regularly, regardless of what we did. Illegal use of drugs was also involved.

Legal authorities became involved, and a judge decided our girl needed to be placed in a juvenile home for correction. His decision and the execution of it was a devastating blow to us and our children. Our position in the college and in the community was severely threatened, and we were filled with guilt over our failure with our daughter. We were soon nervous wrecks over the fear of what would happen to our child.

The court decreed that the married man must never again contact our daughter. However, he continues to communicate with her in the juvenile home and declares they will get back together as soon as she is free. May I please come to see you and receive your prayer and advice?

My Comments

It was at this point the parents came to see me in Ambia, Indiana. They were from strong, conservative, fundamental backgrounds, and had for many years believed in Christ as their Savior. But at this time they were desperate for help and needed a miracle. Most people can rest peacefully in a theology that denies the

4

present miracle-working power of God until they are in deep trouble. Then, they are forced to reach out for new answers.

I explained to them that they first needed to be baptized in the Holy Spirit. This was foreign to everything they had ever been taught, but they wanted to be prayed for. Jesus did baptize them. I then explained that God was using the entire experience their daughter was having and would work it out for her good if they would trust Him.

It was difficult for these parents to be thankful for the problem that they had wrestled so many months trying to solve. But with childlike faith, this professor of philosophy, theology, Hebrew, Greek, and German joined with his wife in thanking God that their entire family had been experiencing exactly what was best for them.

Five weeks later, this couple came back to see me but they were entirely different people. They were bubbling over with joy! They told how their new experience with the Holy Spirit had given them complete peace about their daughter and many other things. One after another, they shared the happy experiences they were having as Jesus became more and more real in their lives. The most exciting thing was what had happened to their daughter. She had gone to a dance at the juvenile home. There she had seen things go on in the rooms adjoining the dance floor that had sickened her. But they were very similar to things she herself had once loved! Something was happening inside of her that she didn't understand. She went back to her room, and for the first time in several years, she prayed. As she did, she was suddenly and powerfully aware of how mixed-up her life had been. She prayed, "God, if You are really alive like my parents say, please help me!"

One after another her sins were poured out to God, and forgiveness filled her heart. She was free. Christ was real! Life was real! Her next letter to her parents told of her growing hunger to be used by God to serve Him in any way He wanted. The man in her life had been contacted and told she now wanted to end their relationship. Through praise, the parents had received from God the gift they had so desperately longed for.

I was speaking in a rather formal church in that area one evening and was inspired by one very happy, glowing face in the front row, the face of a young girl who was so overflowing with joy that she frequently said, "Praise the Lord" in a whisper. She wanted to be "in order," but her joy was so great she could barely contain herself.

At the close of the service, she introduced herself to me, and then it dawned on me that this was the professor's daughter. As her parents had praised God and she had been drawn by the Holy Spirit to accept Christ, I was now being blessed by all of their lives.

Parents, you can cling to your children with all your might, but the day will come when you realize you *have* to turn them over to God so He can be their Father.

"You are to live clean, innocent lives as children of God in a dark world full of people who are crooked and stubborn. Shine out among them like beacon lights, holding out to them the Word of Life" (Phil. 2:15,16 TLB).

LIVED IN HELL

Dear Mr. Carothers,

Mother and I lived in hell because of my alcoholic father. No, I guess we didn't live, we existed. All my life we had little food, lived in the worst shack in town, and lived in fear of what my father might do to us next. In a drunken rage, he would beat my mother and chase me through the house with a belt. I never saw him do a kind thing for Mother in the first thirty years of my life.

When I was twenty-five years old, I accepted Christ and came to know Him in a very real way. Mother had

6

been a Christian for many years. We started praying for my father. After five years of praying, we knew he was worse rather than better. Then I found your book, *Prison to Praise*, in our bookstore. After mother and I had read it, we made a covenant with God to thank Him for my father exactly as he was. That *very night*, my father came home sober for the first time in many years.

He said, "I was walking down the street when a hand came down on my head. I was scared stiff, because I knew it had to be God. He kept His hand on me and wouldn't let go. I knew He was telling me to kneel and pray. I found a place between two buildings and knelt down. My whole life came in front of me, and I was so sick of myself I wanted to vomit. The more I prayed, the happier I got."

Sir, my father hasn't touched a drop since then. Mother acts like she is in heaven, and in a way she is.

My Comments

Please do not expect God to work the same way in every case. He meets each need in the way it needs to be met. His wisdom never errs from absolute perfection. This is considerably different from our wisdom, which has never been perfect even one time!

"O the depth of the riches both of the wisdom and knowledge of God! how unsearchable are his judgments, and his ways past finding out!" (Rom. 11:33).

FROM A MISSIONARY IN VIETNAM

Dear Chaplain Carothers:
While we flew to Saigon on missionary business, we left our son in Nha Trang in the care of a devoted

7

friend. He went with her and other friends to chapel on a Sunday evening. Upon leaving the military chapel, they were driving home when an Army truck driven by a drunken GI swerved into their lane and collided with their car. Our son was killed instantly.

What a shock! What a tragedy! Any normal mother would be crushed. I, too, would have been, had I not learned the blessed secret of praising God. We have realized that our God controls every detail and does all things well. Our son's death is bringing us into deeper, richer, fellowship with Himself and with all the dear ones around us.

At our son's funeral, our missionary family, other missionaries, servicemen, Montagnard teachers, Vietnamese helpers, and local Vietnamese believers stood in sadness, yet acknowledged the truth that was emblazoned over the simple casket: "He lives!!"

After the Army charged the young soldier with manslaughter, the chaplain, at our request, brought him to see us. He entered our home a broken, sobbing man. We shared with him our confidence that our son's death was God's plan for us. We gave him a New Testament and a copy of the most logical book we could think of, your *Prison to Praise*. By the time he left our home, he marveled that God was giving him new strength to face all of us and the future. He acknowledged that he no longer needed to feel desolate, but had been brought to this awful situation to meet God. He had come to say, "I'm sorry," but he parted saying, "Thank you."

After three months of waiting for his trial, the soldier was released and allowed to go home. We saw his birth and growth in Christ during those months, so it all was a great miracle to us. We have had letters from him since his return home, and he is continuing to walk with Christ.

For some time I have wanted to write to you so that you could know how your book, *Prison to Praise*, has been used in the lives of our Wycliffe mission here in Vietnam. Now I have just finished reading *Power in Praise* that a soldier gave to us Sunday. I have already ordered

8

several copies for missionaries here, and I, too, want to study through it again. We saw this new dimension after our son's death, and as you teach, we now want to experience praise daily, even moment by moment by His grace.

My Comments

I shed tears of joy as I read this mother's account of the peace God has given her. God must have rejoiced as He saw her willingness to sacrifice her own son for the salvation of one of God's children. So frequently parents think only of their own grief and shut off love that could save someone else. This mother had every natural reason to despise a drunken soldier, but she loved him for whom Jesus died, and God used her love to continue Christ's work here on earth. This brings the kingdom of God one step closer for all of us!

"In all these things we are more than conquerors through him that loved us. For I am persuaded, that neither death, nor life, nor angels, nor principalities, nor powers, nor things present, nor things to come, nor height, nor depth, nor any other creature, shall be able to separate us from the love of God, which is in Christ Jesus our Lord" (Rom. 8:37-39).

LEGALISM

Dear Colonel Carothers,

I accepted Christ when I was a teen-ager. All along the way I have been troubled by the teachings of legalism. Christ led me into freedom in the Spirit, but I was invited to meet with a charismatic who led me back into even greater legalism. My peace and joy in Christ were soon gone, and I was back to continually fighting the devil, rather than praising God for deliverance through Christ.

When I heard you speak and then read your books, my spirit leaped within me, and I was free again. I never cease to be amazed at the things Christ allows us to get into so He can teach us and bring us into a deeper life with him. Yes, He has even used my backward steps to help me! I spend some time each day with *Power in Praise,* because it lifts me above the problems of this world and fills me with faith in what Christ has done for me.

My Comments

Those who stress legalism do not realize the pain they bring to God's children. They think Christ's perfect peace is only to be realized as we keep His Law. They disregard the reality that none of us can keep His Law. If keeping it was required for us to enter into His Peace, none of us would ever receive His gift to us! None of us have kept Christ's first or second law, and, according to Paul, we haven't even truly wanted to.

We are all so very far from what God wants us to be that we should never tell people they would receive His peace if they would keep His laws like we do. What a contradiction it would be to God's Word if any of us should receive God's gifts by our own efforts rather than through faith in His promises. If well-meaning Christians have caused you to be under the bondage of fear, I exhort you to begin rejoicing in what Jesus has already done for you. He has purchased complete and total peace for you. If you do not receive it, Christ is being cheated out of what He paid for!

"Let me ask you this one question: Did you receive the Holy Spirit by trying to keep the Jewish laws? Of course not, for the Holy Spirit came upon you only after you heard about Christ and trusted him to save you. Then have you gone completely crazy? For it trying to obey the Jewish laws never gave you spiritual life in the first place, why do you think that trying to obey them now will make you stronger Christians?" (Gal. 3:2,3 TLB).

I COULDN'T GROW

Dear Mr. Carothers,

I want to thank the Lord for His inspiration and direction of your life that enabled you to write the book that came my way. In these last few days, my life has begun to change as I have started to try thanking God for everything in my life just as it is.

It is three years since I was baptized in the Holy Spirit, and these last weeks, I have been asking myself and God why I don't lead a more victorious life. The Holy Spirit has told me many times that praising God is the source of all strength and power, but somehow I did not hear Him say, "for everything just as it is."

For years I have found it hard to stay at home and be a homemaker, wife, and mother, and to foster family relationships. My husband and I have even had a separation, and now I see that I wanted him to perform to *my* standard. Now I am thanking God for him, and I am certainly beginning to feel very different: Being free, healed, and knowing that God works constantly for my good and His glory (which are the same) fills me with wonder again and again and floods me with joy.

My Comments

Wanting others to change to fit into our own ideas of what they should be is one of our greatest temptations. When we give them to God in praise, we are free of whatever conflict they may have caused in our lives.

"For whom he did foreknow, he also did predestinate to be conformed to the image of his Son" (Rom. 8:29).

SHOULD I ASK GOD TO CHANGE MY HUSBAND

Dear Chaplain Carothers:

I have read your *Prison to Praise* and *Power in Praise* and enjoyed them very much. You have really helped me a lot. I attend prayer meeting, have been baptized in the Spirit, and speak in tongues. I am happier than I have ever been before, but I have a problem. When you said to praise God in all things, instead of asking Him to take things away, I have been doing just that, because I feel as though God has my life planned.

But I wonder about one thing. Am I supposed to thank God that my husband is living with another woman and that he makes his living being a thief? I have been praising God for this, but what is really bothering me is whether I am ever supposed to pray for him or ask God to show him His love if He already has everyone's life planned for them.

I feel as though I shouldn't ask God for anything like this, because I feel I wouldn't be trusting Him if I did. I guess I am a little bit mixed-up on this, and I thought maybe you would help me.

My Comments

"With thanksgiving let your requests be made known unto God" (Phil. 4:6). We can be thankful because we know God is using the situation, no matter how difficult, to help us and to bless those we love. With this simple faith and trust in Him, we can freely ask for anything we desire. Our faith makes it easy for Him to work. If we come to Him with a fearful or complaining heart, He is unable to give us the desires of our heart.

"If there be any praise, think on these things" (Phil. 4:8).

I WANT TO COME

Dear Brother Carothers,

Truly I thank God for giving you a mind to write such an inspiring book to help many such as I am.

I stopped at my regular bookstore to get a Bible for my foster daughter, and I said to the salesclerk, "I love to read," and she said, "Have you read *Prison to Praise* and *Power in Praise*?"

I said no.

She said, "I have, and am starting to read them over for the second time." She said, "You must read them."

So I thought to myself, "They must really be good," so I bought *Prison to Praise*. Chaplain Carothers, I have no money, but if I did, I would surely ask you to let me come where you are so that you could lay hands on me and pray. For I am in need, so very much, of a touch from the Lord. There seem to be so many things wrong with me, and I feel so out of touch with the Lord. Please pray for me. I feel so heavily burdened down right now. I know the Lord and love the Lord, and I do believe, but yet I doubt, and I hate this in me.

My Comments

You do not have any need to come to me. He has promised to be with you always. Can you believe His promise? Sit down and believe that His hands are resting on you. Your faith releases His power to flow in you. Believe that He meets every need you have and empties you of your doubt and fear. Do not accept doubts, no matter how persistently they try to come into your mind.

"Lo, I am with you alway, even unto the end of the world" (Matt. 28:20).

14

EXPECTING A CHILD

A young couple joyfully looked forward to their first child. A miscarriage brought a painful and abrupt end to their joy. Confusion replaced their youthful faith. "Why had God permitted such a 'wanted child' to be unborn?"

My wife Mary ministered faith to them. "The power of praise works in this too," she assured them. "Let's believe that you will soon have another child. Rejoice and be glad that God has heard your prayers and enjoy expecting the fulfillment of your desires."

Later Mary dreamed that the young wife was expecting and cheerfully looked forward to hearing the announcement. Several weeks passed, but no announcement came. The couple were preparing to leave the area, and in the course of saying good-bye, they said, "Oh, thank you for helping us to believe, so we could have our baby."

"Do you know you are expecting a child again?" Mary exclaimed.

"Oh, yes, didn't you know? We've been sure for several weeks," the young woman replied. The several weeks reached back to the very time that Mary had dreamed of the event being announced!

This power of praise is extremely powerful in bringing to pass the desires of our heart. When we are thanking God for what He is doing, there is no room for any resentment or fear that He is not answering our prayers. If our prayers are for legitimate needs, we have every right to rejoice and be glad that He is meeting our needs. Our rejoicing opens the door wide for Him to walk in and give His personal attention to our specific need. He is a very personal Heavenly Father!

"What things soever ye desire, when ye pray, believe that ye receive them, and ye shall have them" (Mark 11:24).

BROKEN ARM

Dear Rev. Carothers,

Our seven-year-old daughter had an accident at school and severely broke an arm. When we rushed her to the hospital, she was in great pain, and we were naturally extremely anxious for something to to be done for her. When we arrived in the emergency room, the doctor began preparations to set the bone. Before he could begin, a high-school boy was brought in who had broken his arm while playing football. The doctor paused to look at his arm and said, "This boy's arm has a simple fracture that will only take a few minutes to set. I want to set his first."

We went back into the waiting room to wait for our turn. We heard the young man screaming with pain as the doctor worked on him. Naturally, we were fearful of the impact this would have upon our daughter.

To our absolute amazement, she looked at us and said, "He hasn't learned to praise the Lord. I'm thankful for my broken arm, and I believe God will keep me from having pain." She had listened to your tape on praise, and we had started to thank God in our home for little things that happened. But we had no idea that she had completely accepted the idea of praising God for everything. I wondered if this rather unusual experience might shatter her faith. But even as the young man screamed, I could see in my daughter's face that she was at peace and was trusting God.

When we went into the doctor's office, he began to talk to our daughter and explain to her that what he was going to do would hurt her, but that it was necessary to make her arm well.

"No, it won't hurt," she told him. "I've thanked God, and I believe that He is going to keep it from hurting." The doctor gave her a rather sympathetic smile, and when he looked at us, I could tell he was saying, "I am really sorry that I have to be the one to hurt her faith."

As the doctor began working on our daughter's arm, she was relaxed and quiet, with a smile on her face. He would frequently look at her and then at us and shake his head, as if he couldn't understand. Several times he paused and asked, "Does this hurt you very much?"

"No, sir, it doesn't hurt," she quietly responded.

When the surgeon was through, he said, "In all my years of practice, I have never seen anything like this."

Before this experience, our daughter had always been very normal in experiencing pain. This was the very first time that she responded in any unusual way. We can clearly see that God worked one of His blessed miracles for our daughter. She may not always be free of pain, but she will always remember this incident where God honored her faith as she praised Him. Thank you for teaching us this wonderful secret of the power of praise.

My Comments

God has not promised to always protect us from pain, but He has promised to honor our faith. When little children are led into the teachings of praising God, their simple faith will reach out and grasp God's great power. If you find that your own faith is weak, I suggest that you find little children. Teach them what the Bible says about praising God in everything, and then watch to see how they are able to release their faith. Their faith will strengthen yours, and together you will see what God will do.

"A little child shall lead them" (Isa. 11:6).

WHY?

Dear Sir,

If God is really alive, why does He permit such horrible things to happen, such as six million Jews to be tortured and killed during World War II? Doesn't He care about the millions who are now starving to death? Is He so holy that He doesn't care about all the people who are suffering in the world? Do you really thank God that all of these terrible things are going on?

My Comments

God gave man the right to rule over the earth and everything in it. God made it this way and told man that it would be this way as long as the world existed. God could not and did not lie to us. This world is ours to do with as we will. He will intervene only through our faith in Him. You do not have this faith in Him, and He therefore cannot change anything through your faith.

You should do something about the wrong things in the world yourself! Do you think you as one person are unable to do anything? The evils you speak about are usually caused by one man. One man usually has to be the source behind everything. Edison, Napoleon, Alexander the Great, and Lincoln did what they wanted to do. They came into the world with the same power you did. God gives you the freedom to do whatever good you want to do if you have the desire to do it.

Finding fault with "what is" always takes less energy than doing something about it. Hitler dedicated his entire life to doing what he wanted to do. No man should complain about the way God has made the world until he has done his best to change it for the better. If you are a complainer, remember that God has promised to help you do anything good you set your heart to.

"What is the exceeding greatness of his power to us-ward who believe!" (Eph. 1:19-23). "Ours is not a conflict with mere flesh and blood, but with the despotisms; the empires, the forces that control and govern this dark world, the spiritual hosts of evil arrayed against us in heavenly warfare" (Eph. 6:12 Weymouth).

"Behold I have given you authority ... over all the power of the enemy" (Luke 10:19 TLB).

WITH PAT BOONE

My wife Mary and I were enjoying the atmosphere of joy and peace in Pat Boone's very comfortable home in Beverly Hills, California. As we were seated in their living room chatting, beyond Shirley and Pat lay the swimming pool in which over 300 persons have been baptized into Christ. We were thrilled as Pat, in a very simple, sincere manner, talked of his growing faith in Christ. He recounted one incident after another in which he had enjoyed the opportunity to share with others his new walk in Christ and the power of the Holy Spirit. I felt my heart being warmed as I saw how dedicated he was to sharing his love for Christ with people in all walks of life. One after another he told of people's lives that had been transformed as a result of reading *Prison to Praise*.

Shirley Boone bubbled over with enthusiasm as she told how learning to praise God had brought such strength to her, and how God had brought this insight to her at just the right time.

"I was in the midst of the most trying experiences of my life," she said. She went on to list these experiences and how God had lifted her burdens as she thanked Him. There is one incident I would like to share.

One night when Pat was out of town, Shirley was at home alone with the children. In the middle of the night, the house began to shake.

"Earthquakes have always been my most passionate fear," Shirley explained. "I have frequently urged Pat to move us away from this area, because of my persistent fear. As I awakened, I realized we were having the worst earthquake I had ever experienced. I bounded out of bed. When I hit the floor, I did an amazing thing. I said, and felt, 'Praise the Lord. Thank You for this earthquake!' It was a spontaneous response, an overflow of what I had been continually practicing for several months. I headed for the children's rooms while I literally bounced off the walls as the house was violently shaken. This earthquake in 1971 was one of Los Angeles' worst. When I reached the girls, I urged them to join me in thanking God for the earthquake! We had absolutely no fear and praised God for His protecting care.

"Following the quake, the psychiatrists were kept very busy with distraught and fear-filled children from the Hollywood area. They reported that the children were more upset by the fear shown by their parents than they were by the earthquake itself! Our united praise destroyed all power that fear might otherwise have brought into our home."

During the conversation, the Boones joyfully shared how visitors had commented on entering their home, "There is something different in this house. There is a feeling of peace. What is it?"

There is a secret presence of rest there, that the Spirit of Jesus brings with Him. The Scripture tells us of a sweet aroma of His presence. This peace brings rest that the most carefully designed atmosphere can never duplicate. The spirit of man longs to enter into rest, and God alone is able to supply that need. We have a God-designed vacuum within us that can be filled only by His Spirit. Elaborate, beautiful homes, elegant furnishings, and costly decorations may at first appearance seem to be the source of inward rest, but prolonged living in such settings reveals the eternal truth that only Jesus brings peace. Lean back in your cracked, creaking, torn, and ancient relic of a chair and laugh inside if Jesus is there in your home. If He is, you have the most blessed home on the block. If you are thrashing around in discontent and complaining, your physical surroundings are not your problem. You have a hole inside that only Jesus can fill with peace.

"I will fear no evil: for thou art with me" (Ps. 23:4).

EYE SURGERY

Dear Mr. Carothers,

No words in the English language can describe the feeling I had inside of me when I read your book, *Prison to Praise*. I felt closer to the Divine Lord than ever before. I myself had a very special intention last week. My teacher, who let me read your marvelous book, had a very serious eye operation. If the surgery did not prove to be successful, she would be totally blind. My friend and I thanked the Lord and prayed very hard for her—and last Friday morning, the phone rang to say she could see again. This brightened my heart more than anything on the whole earth.

By the way, my teacher is a Roman Catholic nun. Your book taught me a new method of praising the Lord and a wonderful one, too. One of my greatest wishes is that I can meet you someday and talk to you. I am in the seventh grade in grammar school in Rochester. Your book has influenced my life so much that you are God's prophet to me. May the Heavenly Father send His perpetual blessing down on your head and your family, too. Please write back—I'd love to have you as my Christ friend!

My Comments

With young people like this in our country, we have great prospects. God is bringing new faith into their

21

hearts, and they are believing His simple promises. If the young people you know are not as loving and Jesus-centered as this seventh-grade student, you can help them. This teacher gave her students a book, and God used the book to help meet her need.

"Dear brothers, what's the use of saying that you have faith and are Christians if you aren't proving it by helping others?" (James 2:14 TLB).

WRONG NAME

Dear Rev. Carothers,

I believe you. Praise is the answer. When I read your book, I started to praise God all the time. I noticed that I began to feel better than I ever had. I'm a businessman, and I know enough to hold on to something if it works. The atmosphere in our home started changing, and everyone was happier than we had ever been before.

My brother was driving to Southern California to visit us and was involved in a minor car accident. A man had backed into the front of his car and damaged his radiator and fan enough that the car wouldn't work. The man causing the accident had given my brother his name, address, and driver's license number. My brother called me and asked if I could come to Los Angeles and pull his car to our home. I left as soon as I found a tow bar, but en route realized he had only given me the street in Los Angeles that he was on, and the street was at least twenty-five miles long. I was driving on a thruway into Los Angeles and decided which exit would be best to take to begin looking for him. When I came to this exit, the traffic was so solid on the right lane that I couldn't get over to leave the thruway. The old me would have grumbled, but I started praising the Lord that I couldn't get into the right lane! By the next exit into Los Angeles, I still couldn't find an opening to turn right. I praised the Lord! Another exit came, and still I couldn't get over. By the next exit, I was able to get over, so I praised the Lord for this and believed God would work it out that I hadn't passed the place where my brother might be.

When I reached the end of the exit ramp, I could hardly believe my eyes! There was my brother standing beside his car!

We pulled the car to our home, and the next day I tried to telephone the man who had hit my brother's car to find out about his insurance. The operator said there was no one listed by the name my brother had been given, and there was no such address as the one he had been given. I went to a friend who was a policeman and asked him to check on the driver's license number to see who it belonged to. He discovered the license number was fictitious! My brother hadn't asked to see the license for himself.

By this time, my brother's anger was rising. I said, "No, that isn't the solution. I've learned from Chaplain Carothers that we are supposed to thank the Lord for everything, so I am thanking Him that the man tricked you." My brother reacted as if he thought I had become a religious nut of some kind.

We went to a junkyard to try to buy an inexpensive radiator off an old car. The dealer said he had one, but had sold it only an hour earlier. Again my brother cursed his bad luck. I said, "Praise the Lord, this is what was supposed to happen." Then I was inspired to say, "Let's believe that God is going to work something better out."

When we got home, my wife said a man had made a person-to-person call for my brother. He returned the call, and guess who was calling? My brother had given the man who hit him our telephone number, and he had called. He said, "I apologize for giving you the wrong name and address. I've been feeling guilty about it, and I want to make it right." And he did!

My Comments

Isn't it wonderful to be on the side of a God who keeps His promises to us? The odds of a man who would be dishonest enough to give a wrong name and address, and then be honest enough to call and give his right name, are very small. But our God does not deal with odds. He has promised to work out everything for good if we trust Him. I was able to visit this family in California, and had the joy of hearing this businessman tell how this incident had caused his brother to accept Christ!

God works in all things as we learn to trust Him. Evidence is piling up all over the world that God is moving in every possible way to draw the final number of men into His kingdom before the return of His Son. You can be a part of this mighty force God is using. Dedicate your life to praising God for everything. He will use your praise to win others to Christ. Is it worth this to you? The side benefit is that God will fill your whole life with the perfect peace and joy that Jesus promised to give.

"The Lord is not slack concerning his promise, as some men count slackness; but is longsuffering to us-ward, not willing that any should perish, but that all should come to repentance" (II Pet. 3:9).

I HAD IT MADE

Dear Mr. Carothers,

I had it made, but I didn't know it. Life was very simple and beautiful at our middle-class home, and I know now that my mother and father really loved me. I graduated from high school with the usual rounds of parties, fun, and games. My boyfriend was a basketball star, so we got in on all the "best things." High school wasn't the most fun, but I enjoyed it more than some kids did. My parents gave me a hard time about coming in late at night, and I resented this, but they gave me everything I needed and more besides. In addition to all of this, I received a scholarship to a very good college.

Everything looked like roses—until I discovered I was pregnant. Then the roof fell in. My hero boyfriend said he wasn't ready to get married yet, because he couldn't afford it. I recognized the movie plot, and didn't want to see him ever again. When I told my parents my problem, they didn't blow up, but they made it plain that I had ruined the reputation of the whole family. They wanted me to go to visit a distant relative, if you know what I mean.

I wanted to die, and thought of all the ways I could. Day after day I stayed in my room trying to figure out what to do. Finally, I decided to do one of two things: Get a job and earn enough money so I could go and get an abortion, or decide on some method of suicide. Every hour I changed my mind.

Then one day my parents came to my room with a book. They said it had changed their whole attitude about what had happened to me. They wanted me to stay at home to have the baby, and they wanted me to believe they were glad I was pregnant! I thought something had blown their minds. They asked me to read your book, *Prison to Praise*. At first, I couldn't figure out why they wanted me to read it. But the last two chapters were like a message from heaven when I read them. I laughed, and I cried, and I asked God to forgive me for wanting to take my life. And I knew He had forgiven me already.

My parents had taken me to church until I was a senior in high school, but when I made a big fuss about it, they finally let me quit. I asked them what going to church had ever done for us, and they couldn't give me any good answer.

But after reading your book, I *wanted* to go to church. I wanted to find out about the baptism in the Holy Spirit that you wrote about. I asked about it at church, but no one seemed to know anything about it. Then one night we went to a Full Gospel Business Men's Fellowship meeting, and to my astonishment, you were there! I knew this had to be a miracle. I went forward when you invited us, and God really did something to me. He really did!

Things may be a little difficult for me yet, but now I can honestly thank the Lord for all that has happened to me. He has helped me in a way I would never have even wanted before. I thank the Lord for *Prison to Praise*. When you write anything more, please let me know.

My Comments

A conventional, comfortable life with everything in neat respectable order may seem to be ideal, but God knows more about our actual needs than we will ever know here in this life. He will override our self-satisfaction and complacency and put us in positions where we will have to let the Holy Spirit meet our needs through Christ. The blessedness of this is that He also makes *this* life better than ever before! Praise the Lord!

"I am come that they might have life, and that they might have it more abundantly" (John 10:10).

I AM IN JAIL

Dear Merlin,

I am in jail. During my first week here, I couldn't understand why God did it to me. I was terribly unhappy, and didn't believe that God or people were trying to help me. Then one of the guards gave me a little book, called *Prison to Praise*, and I read it. Partway through, I tried to pray and when I prayed, my words became all mixed-up, and I realized that I was praying in another language. But this is not the strangest part of what happened.

I found out later that while I was in jail, my wife decided to go to church with someone who had invited her. I'm sure that she never would have gone if I had been at home. While she was there, she was filled with the Holy Spirit and spoke in other tongues. We have now discovered that she and I began speaking in a new language at exactly the same time. I can see how God used putting me into jail, someone giving me your book, and then did something great for us. It has helped me realize that all the aches and pains we go through are for a purpose. Each day I am growing stronger in the Lord. Everything He does is good. I shall keep on praising Jesus and God. I say, "Thank You, God, for making Merlin the way he is." You've helped me a lot. God bless you.

My Comments

In that same jail, I am sure there are many men who are filled with bitterness. The same bars God has used to bring you joy are turning their lives into hate. God is using books like *Prison to Praise* and many others to break through prison walls into places where His people may not easily go. You have the opportunity to break into many prisons and to turn darkness into light.

Remember Jesus' exhortation, "to go into prisons and hospitals in His name." The needs were never greater, the opportunities were never more abundant, nor the blessings greater, than they are today.

"I the Lord have called thee in righteousness ... to bring out the prisoners from the prison, and them that sit in darkness out of the prison house" (Isa. 42:6,7).

STATE POLICEMAN

Dear Chaplain Carothers,

I want to share with you what God did for me as a result of your visit to our church. I am a thirty-year-old State Policeman and a former serviceman.

You spoke on, "In all things give thanks!" I was very impressed with your message, and so came forward when you issued a prayer call. I had been praying that God would remove the doubt that was in my heart and replace it with faith. Even though so many things had already happened, the devil kept putting doubt in my mind. I thought, "Am I really a Christian or just pretending to be?"

You laid your hand on me to pray. The next thing I remember is coming back to consciousness while lying on the floor. When I first saw people falling under the power of God, I said, "Not me, baby!" But here I was. Everybody was so joyous and having a wonderful time, which is the way it should be. We have something great to be proud of.

My Comments

God is touching people in every walk of life. It is awesome to see people being made unconscious by the Holy Spirit. In my early ministry, I was convinced that only highly emotional people became so excited in the church that they passed out. God has proved how wrong I was.

My wife Mary and I were eating during a FGBMFI banquet when I said to her, "Wouldn't it be great if God would strike people down like He did in John Wesley's ministry?" At the end of my message, and at the close of my invitation for people to come forward, I was led of the Spirit to say, "There is a man here who has been hearing about the Holy Spirit but has been fighting it off. He has been unwilling to let the Holy Spirit fill him. He should stand up now."

A man stood up immediately and came forward. When he reached the altar, he collapsed in front of the speaker's table as if he had been hit by a ball bat. Several men picked him up and set him on a chair. When they let go of him, he fell to the floor again. I confess that I thought, "This must be a very emotional Pentecostal, who has learned to expect such things." (The Lord has forgiven me for thinking this.)

Later, I prayed with the man, and he stood up laughing and praising the Lord for filling him with the Holy Spirit. He was freely praying in a new language.

After the meeting, I asked one of the men who the brother was who came forward. He said, "He is an Episcopalian who works for the government. Do you know him?"

The man gave his name, and I said, "No, I don't recognize the name." Then they explained that he was the top laser-beam expert in the entire United States! He didn't fit the category I had tried to place him in.

Since then, I've seen some of the most unemotional businessmen being struck to the floor by the Holy Spirit, but in every case it has not been a demonstration of

God's anger, but of His Spirit touching man to reveal God's great love. The power of His love is actually so strong that a small flow causes the human brain to go into unconsciousness. When the person comes to, he nearly always says something like, "I feel as if every part of me, inside and out, has been washed clean. I feel glorious!"

But you do not need to be made unconscious to feel the power of God's love. Do not even seek for such outward signs. He wants you to believe He loves you even as you read this. Believe that He washes you completely clean by His love.

"For God so loved the world, that he gave his only begotten Son, that whosoever believeth in him should not perish, but have everlasting life" (John 3:16).

A PROFESSOR SPEAKS OUT

Dear Brother Carothers,

Thanks for your address at our college alumni banquet, and for the books God inspired you to write. The speech left me thinking you had a wonderful theme, but I thought some statements were extreme. Although my wife had copies of your books, it was several months before I started reading them. When I read *Power in Praise*, I thought, "This is unscriptural. It makes God the author of evil." But I turned to the book, *Prison to Praise,* and began to ponder more deeply. My prejudice began to melt away.

Finally, I took a big step of faith and began thanking God for making me as He did, physically and in every way, weaknesses and all. As a result, I felt unusually happy all day. In the evening, I looked across the room at my wife and thanked God for giving me such a wife with just her peculiarities and faults. I got blessed again. Next day I wrote in my diary, "It is high time that I was rid of resentment over the mistakes I make. 'Woe to him who strives with his Maker, an earthen vessel with the Potter!' I thank God for my humanity. 'Will what is molded say to its Molder, Why have You made me thus?' I fear that is what I have done, more or less all my life. What folly!"

Later, while working at my desk and vexing myself, as usual, over the errors I was making, I stopped, looked up, and said firmly, "Well, thank the Lord for the mistakes!" At last, in my seventieth year of life, I saw that my errors were one means the Lord was using to humble me and get me to rely more completely on Him. From that, it was just a step to including the whole panorama of God's providences in one grand sweep of praise.

The result was marvelous. Joy and peace flooded my soul. Hidden pride had given way to a new sense of God's love and power. I began to accept people more readily. Blessing began flowing out to them more fully. In a matter of days, two of our daughters, both of them ministers' wives, prayed through to greater victory than they had ever known before. I am experiencing more faith and love in praying for others.

May the Lord continue to use you in a marvelous way. I thank the Lord for your faithful ministry. It is a wonderful day in which to live and serve. Praise the *Lord!*

My Comments

Any comments on this beautiful letter would be superfluous. Long before I received this letter, I considered this professor to be one of the finest Christian gentlemen I have ever known. He is a well-educated professor of history at a conservative Christian college, an author highly respected among his peers.

"He that humbleth himself shall be exalted" (Luke 14:11).

BACK HEALED

My dear Brother Carothers,

Thanks for your letter. Yes, God healed me just a short time after I received your book, *Prison to Praise.* I had been having trouble with my back for many years.

As I was reading about how we should praise the Lord at all times, regardless of circumstances, the Lord suddenly told me if I would raise my hands and praise Him, He would heal me. I immediately obeyed the Lord, and was instantly delivered. Oh, how I praise the Lord Jesus Christ for His goodness to us!

Surely Jesus is the Answer today and every day. I love Him with all my heart.

Your book, *Prison to Praise,* is a testimony of what Christ can do. Truly Jesus deserves all our praise each day. I have been passing your book around to the neighbors.

My Comments

Have you heard the expression, "If it works, don't knock it"? Hundreds of people tell me about healings that come when they believe God is using their infirmity for some useful purpose. This has to be a "heart belief," and the Holy Spirit gives us this kind of faith. For this reason, none of us dare boast about "our" great faith.

———

"Even trusting is not of yourselves; it too is a gift from God" (Eph. 2:8 TLB).

CHILD LOSING HALF HER FOOT

Dear Sir,

I have been a Christian for fifteen years but really haven't done much growing. Now I know that I must experience the baptism in the Holy Spirit. My desire is very strong, and I have asked the Lord to lead me to someone who can help me.

One thing that has brought me to the present position is what has happened to my granddaughter. She was born with a birth defect in her left foot. Her circulation is very bad. She has had surgery, and the foot has gone from bad to worse. She has been in a great deal of pain, with ulcers on the top and bottom of the foot. Six vascular specialists have seen her, and they have all come to the same conclusion—to remove the toe and part of the foot to the end of her arch. I tremble just writing this.

When my son called to tell me about it, I cried all day and told the Lord that if He didn't have any more mercy than this, I didn't want Him for my God. I had been praying for my granddaughter since she was born, and had prayed that God would heal her. I couldn't believe that He would do this to her. For four days I couldn't pray, but the last two of those days I really felt His closeness and felt held up by the prayers of my friends and my church. Then a friend gave me your book to read. Chaplain, I want to tell you that a wonderful feeling of faith came into me, and I now believe that God is working out some very wonderful plan.

Dear Christian friend,

There is a great difference between believing that God is using all things for good and in believing that God causes things. I do not believe that God has caused this disease in your granddaughter. The devil is the author of all sickness and pain. God has only promised to take all sickness and work it for good if we will trust Him.

In this case, it is already evident that God has used her pain to draw you to Himself. Unfortunately, it often takes pain in our own bodies, or pain in our loved ones, to help us to realize how much we need His help. Many people are content to live with a powerless faith until they need urgent positive help. Then they cry out to God and want whatever He has that will bring an answer. Learning to believe and trust God is not something that we latch hold of at the moment we think we need it. It takes much learning to get rid of our fears and natural distrust of faith.

I surely am joining in prayer that God will touch your granddaughter, heal her foot, and bless her life for His glory.

My Comments

When there is potential rebellion in our hearts against God, it is a loving God who permits incidents to happen that show us what is inside. We could go on for the rest of our life believing that we had a perfectly pure heart, until God lets things happen to show us how rebellious we can be. It is for our good. Instead of responding in fear or anger, we should respond in faith and trust. Tragedies teach us the important secrets of how to trust and believe in God.

"Ye that fear the Lord, praise him" (Ps. 22:23).

MISSIONARY TO THE UNITED STATES

Chaplain Carothers,

For over two years, I have been a very sick woman, nearly dying three times. It has been a time of great trial, and I have wished many times I could go home to be with my Lord.

About a month ago I had another bad spell and was in bed for eight days. One evening, a young man who worships in our church put into my hands a book.

"Try and read it," he said. The next morning, I was rather distressed and weeping. I heard God say to me, "Why don't you praise Me for it?"

"How can I praise You in such a state?" I asked. At that moment I saw your book, *Prison to Praise*.

God said, "Go ahead and read it," so I picked it up and started to read. Dear Brother, I just wept for joy. Here was my answer. I had thanked God for my healing, but could not understand how to rid myself of the symptoms. Oh glory! In one hour I was up praising God, and He commenced my healing. Slowly He is making me whole. Bless His lovely name.

I have read and reread your book, and the more I do, the more I see how stupid Christians are. I love the way you jumped up and down and said, "I love you." I, too, have done this many times. It's wonderful isn't it?

I have found not many can take this. They prefer the old way, being dressed in Satan's shroud, but I will now be dressed in God's praises.

I have been to your land twice as a missionary, once to Arizona and then later to California. I loved it and hope one day God will let me come again.

My Comments

When symptoms persist, it is natural to think, "I must not be healed." But God wants us to believe Him regardless of any pain or discomfort we may feel. "When your patience is finally in full bloom, then you will be ready for anything" (James 1:4 TLB).

It is amazing to me that some would prefer to be miserable and unhappy rather than give in to God's exhortation to praise Him. I have known many people who actually were angry and distressed at my urgings to praise God. They determined to be unhappy if it killed them. And sure enough, their anger is slowly killing them.

"Yes, I will bless the Lord and not forget the glorious things he does for me. He forgives all my sins. He heals me" (Ps. 103:2,3 TLB).

YOUNG MOTHER LOVES TEEN-AGE ADDICT

Dear Rev. Carothers,

I am the mother of three small children and have more than enough to keep me busy. But the first time I saw this teen-age girl, my heart went right out to her. I wanted to put my arms around her and tell her I loved her.

When I asked others about this girl, they said everyone had given up on her. She had made many promises to kick the drug habit, but had always gone right back to drugs. People were really tired of her lying so much. But I felt an even greater love for this girl and began to patiently show her all the love and affection I could.

Giving love to others had always been very easy to me. It seemed very natural for me to love people. I loved this teen-age addict with very little effort, even when others told me I was wasting my time. But I did have one problem. I was critical of those who were critical of others! I couldn't see why so many Christians wanted to consistently judge other Christians. I kept thinking, "Why don't they love people? I'm not a perfect Christian, but at least I love people as they are." When I saw other Christians showing a lack of warmth, I thought, "If we can't even love other Christians, how can we even claim to be Christian?"

As the teen-age girl became more and more unreceptive to my love, I responded by being more patient and more loving. But one evening I looked at this girl at a time when she was being especially obnoxious and was aware that I was completely exhausted. Weeks of effort to break through her sullen barrier had worn down all my reserve strength. I no longer wanted to have anything to do with her! I wanted her out of my life. It was evident to me that I had nothing more to give her.

When I next met this young girl, it was in church. I tried to hide the new feelings I had, but I couldn't. The girl turned from me, and I knew she wouldn't be coming back to me for help. And something else was going on in me at the same time. I was becoming very critical of many other people. I saw faults, weaknesses, and failures in people whom I had known and loved for years. Guilt mounted up as I realized I was doing the very same thing I had so disliked in others! I became more and more aware that I had hurt the young girl and was now starting to dislike even my best friends. When I prayed for God to take away this unloving spirit, nothing happened.

I then read your book on being thankful for everything. I thought, "How could I possibly be thankful for my terrible attitude?" But I decided to try anyhow. As I thanked the Lord for myself exactly as I was, the aching burden lifted! I was free. "But why have I become so critical of others?" I asked God.

"You had been thinking that it was your own love that loved people. You were taking the credit for loving

37

the unlovely when it was My Son loving them through you."

All I could think of was, "Oh, yes, Lord. I believe You. I criticized others for being unloving when I should have been asking You to love through them".

As this confession came from me, I experienced a physical warming of my entire body. Love for others flowed back into me. It was much stronger than it had ever been. The very next time I saw the teen-age girl, I knew that I loved her far more than I ever had. Only this time, I knew I was loving with Jesus' love.

My Comments

This mother is now a radiant witness to the grace of God. My own life and ministry were blessed by the discoveries she made. She proved that being thankful even for our own weaknesses and failures opens the door for God to teach us how dependent we are upon Him for any goodness in ourselves. Self-righteousness is a vice that God looks upon with anger, and I long to be rid of all of it. Whenever I lose even one little critical attitude toward others, I quickly respond with, "Thank You, Lord, for helping me. I know I couldn't have done it myself."

"Judge not, that ye be not judged. For with what judgment ye judge, ye shall be judged" (Matt. 7:1,2).

LOST CONTACT LENS

Dear Chaplain Carothers,

I'm a thirteen-year-old boy who heard your talk on praising God. I've heard many times about praising God,

38

but never about praising Him for the bad things that happen. But when I heard you speak, I decided you must be right.

I started to thank God for the little things I didn't really like, and I seemed to feel much better about everything. One evening it was nearly zero outside, and it had started to snow very hard. I had to run outdoors to get something out of our car, and as I closed the car door, I bumped my head. One of my contact lenses fell into the snow. Before I could look for it, I needed to get a coat on, so I went inside and told Mother what had happened. At first she was getting real upset. I told her I was praising the Lord, for I knew He had some good reason for letting it happen. She agreed with me and calmed down. But when I started to go outside to look for the lens, she laughed and said there wasn't any chance at all of finding the contact lens in the dark with snow falling.

"I believe the Lord will help me find it," I said.

I took a flashlight with me, and guess what happened! In less than five minutes I found the lens. I *know* God did this for me, and that He wanted to teach me to trust Him. I'm praising Him more than ever now.

My Comments

God's "little people" can often lead us in learning to trust Him. They are not hindered by the heavy weights that often hold our faith down. But we, too, can become "like little children" and with joy face each new problem with faith that He will provide the perfect solution.

———————

"With God all things are possible" (Matt. 19:26).

OUT OF WORK

Dear Sir,

My brother has been out of work for a year. Unlike many people, he really wants a job. He has no special skill, and would be willing to do anything in order to support his family. He has a wife and two children, and he is ashamed that he has been on welfare for so long. Since he is not a Christian, I have not suggested that he thank God for his problem, but I've been wondering if it would do him any good. I asked him to read *Prison to Praise*, but he wouldn't read it. I'm thanking God that he doesn't have a job, but nothing seems to happen. Do you have any suggestions?

Dear Sister,

God has not given His special promise, of working everything out for good, to your brother, since he does not love God. He does not want God's help. But the grace of God is even beyond what He has promised to do. Challenge your brother with the stories you have read in my books, and ask him to at least give praise a chance. If you are bold enough with him, he might take it as a dare to give God a chance. I'll be believing with you that God will reach him through you.

Dear Sir,

I prayed and then did what you suggested. I told my brother about Ray and Sue and about the man whose furnace went out, and then I nearly dared him to thank God that he didn't have a job. To my surprise, he said, "Okay, I'll do it!"

The next morning my brother had to take one of his children to the doctor. He was ashamed that he couldn't pay the bill, so he asked the doctor if he could do anything to work for his fees. The doctor said no, but he had a friend who needed a man to work for him, and would call the friend if my brother honestly wanted a job.

Rev. Carothers, he got the job! He came home that night nearly in a state of shock. "It works!" he said. "I want to read that book you told me about."

He read *Prison to Praise* all that evening and then made this marvelous simple announcement: "I want to be a Christian."

My Comments

Praising God is not limited to any certain kind of people. Results of some kind will always be realized. A materially minded man may get only material results, but if his heart is open, God will speak to him through the material things he understands, and draw him to Christ. The law of gravity works for all men, and the law of praise does exactly the same thing. The exact results of praise may not be so easily predictable as gravity, but results are sure.

"On that day you will say, 'Praise the Lord,' He was angry with me, but now he comforts me!" (Isa. 12:1 TLB).

PASTOR BAPTIZED

Dear Merlin,

When the people in my church started urging me to "Praise the Lord," I responded with antagonism. It seemed to me they were saying they were closer to God than I, their pastor, was. Their new enthusiasm pleased me, but also made me fearful they were emphasizing emotion too much. When I heard they were also speaking in tongues, I knew it was time for them to change their ways or find a new church.

One of this group asked me to read your two books. I agreed, thinking it would be easier for me to argue with them if I knew what they were reading. When I finished reading, I agreed to attend one of their meetings, but I didn't go to argue. I was experiencing a desire to find out if their experience and yours was what I had been needing all my life. You will probably understand what I am saying if I tell you I left that meeting, a man with a "silly grin."

My Comments

Laymen all over the world are being undampered by their minister's lack of understanding. They are loving him, sharing, and believing that God will meet his needs through them. It often takes a while for the minister to see the real blessing he has been missing, but when he does, the kingdom of God has a new man with a "silly grin."

"And everyone present was filled with the Holy Spirit and began speaking in languages they didn't know, for the Holy Spirit gave them this ability. . . . Crowds came running to see what it was all about. . . . They stood there amazed and perplexed. 'What can this mean?' they asked each other.

"But others in the crowd were mocking. 'They're drunk, that's all!' they said" (Acts 2:4,6,12,13 TLB).

WHICH DENOMINATION?

Dear Brother Carothers,

I have just been reading your book, *Prison to Praise*. Where I go to church, they think that all others of other faiths are hell-bound. They wear no makeup, and let their hair grow long and straight. Most of them are so narrow-minded, they can't see God moving in other faiths. They try to clean up the outward appearance and don't try to clean up the inward man.

I thank God He has begun to open up my eyes to a wider look, to clean up the inward man for Him and still look good on the outside, too, for my husband. I thank and praise God so much for all the things He is doing for all men, not just men of one faith. I read your book a little and cried and praised God and read a little more. I thank God for the friend who let me read the book. I had heard so much about it. I have heard teen-agers talk about it on the radio, how they read the book and were healed of spine trouble.

My Comments

Last night I stood in a church filled with people from a denomination which had been traditionally known as one of the most formal, liberal churches in our country. As they worshiped God in praise, their hands were uplifted, and tears of joy were flowing down their faces. As they sang, there was a radiant glow. The entire service manifested the mighty power of love for one another. There were several testimonies of divine healing, being filled with the Holy Spirit, and of deliverance from all kinds of problems. The name of Jesus was mentioned over and over. In the congregation, I saw several nuns, at least one priest of the Roman Catholic church, several hippie types, and many well-dressed, successful people.

God in His love, is moving upon all flesh; denominational barriers are being broken down. Those who have looked upon themselves as being "the only true church" are rapidly discovering the joy of knowing God's children in other denominations.

"Sanctify them through thy truth: thy word is truth" (John 17:17).

DOPE

Chaplain Carothers,

You don't know me, but I just finished reading your book, *Prison to Praise*, and the spiritual knowledge I gained from it equals no other book I've read, except the Bible itself. Presently I am in the Kern County jail, awaiting trial for possession of marijuana and dangerous drugs. The last eighteen months I've spent in a correctional institution for heroin addiction. I have finally awakened to the fact that only through the grace of God and through His will can I ever be totally cured of my narcotic problem. I am twenty-one years old, and a Christian of only four weeks. While reading your book, I wanted to break down and cry, something I thought I'd forgotten how to do. I've told our Lord that I'm *all* His, problems and all, and I've prayed that He will answer my prayers and guide me in the years to come.

Yet somehow I feel I'm still missing something, but I can't seem to put my finger on it. I would appreciate it very much if you would remember me in your prayers, as you have the power of the Holy Ghost in you. I have to close here, so thank you for your book, your time, and may God continue to bless you.

My Comments

Here is a striking example of the power in the printed testimony. We can reach behind prison bars and bring new hope to men if we care about them. In Illinois, there is an organized effort to get Christian books into the hands of the men in prison. Perhaps you could organize the churches, civic groups, and clubs in your community to canvass the entire area to find good books to supply to the men in the prisons near you. Better yet, you could select the books you know will help men the most, and then collect money to buy these books for the prisoners. They have days and days with nothing to do but stare at the bare walls. They *feel* like animals and come out *acting like* animals. You could put books into their hands that will change their lives and lead them to eternal life.

Jesus said to visit the men in prisons. You have the potential of visiting hundreds through the printed page! But please do not send the traditional tracts or books on repentance. They know they are bad. They need to know what God will do for them.

"I the Lord have called thee . . . to open the blind eyes, to bring out the prisoners from the prison, and them that sit in darkness out of the prison house" (Isa. 42:6,7).

MINISTER MOVES

Some ministers, like many men in other professions, have to move more frequently than they would like to. A Methodist minister received a change of assignment and came home to break the news to his wife and two teen-age daughters, who reacted with a flood of anguished tears. They could accept having to move, but the assignment they received was to the worst place in the entire district. Every minister's family in the district prayed that they would never have to go to "that place." Every member of the family was unhappy about the move.

But they had to pack up and go, tears or no tears. Six years later, the family rejoiced, agreeing that this assignment had been the most blessed experience in all their lives. In every possible way, this parish had fulfilled each of them in such a complete way that they knew God had planned for them to be there. As they looked back, they couldn't help but think what a waste their tears of self-pity had been. God had not forsaken them or forced unpleasant experiences upon them. They had failed to understand that God was working in their life to bless them.

My Comments

It may take more or less than six years for you to know what He is doing to bless you, but go ahead and trust now. Let Him reveal the purpose later.

"Those who sow tears shall reap joy" (Ps. 126:5 TLB).

DIVORCE

Dear Merlin,

I finally received your book, *Power in Praise*, and since reading it and *Prison to Praise*, I seem to be so full of joy that I carry a song in my heart. I do thank you for writing them.

I have been through two divorces (the last, ten years ago) and suppose I have been resenting that I've never found marital happiness, although I have been very blessed in other ways. I've raised two sons alone for twenty years and managed to get them through college. Both are naval officers and pilots and are now married and very fine young men.

Since reading your books, I'm thanking God for all I've been through and know it is part of my Divine plan. I feel now I will find the right companion in marriage. Please write to me when you have the time and teach me exactly how to pray about this and a daughter-in-law who gives us much trouble.

My Comments

Divorce, like other experiences in life, is often a very painful thing. But God has promised to use all things for our good, if we trust Him and praise Him. This woman is realizing the power that is released when she trusts God to take her life's experiences and work them out for something good.

I advised her that no earthly person could teach us how to pray in some specific problem. The ministry of the Holy Spirit is to teach us what to pray and how to pray.

"We know not what we should pray for as we ought: but the Spirit itself maketh intercession for us" (Rom. 8:26).

NO JOY

Dear Chaplain Carothers,

I have read your book, *Prison to Praise*, three times. Each time, I have tried to find within myself the reason why I don't have the joy that you have expressed in your book.

I have a deep hunger for a closer walk with God. But for some reason I can't seem to find the fulfillment I need. Can you help me by mail?

Our home is a new Christian home. We are a retired Air Force family. We have shared many problems that face the military. But the life in Christ has brought new problems that I am not able to cope with in victory. I feel a Christian must live a victorious life. But something is missing.

Thank you for your book, for it has let me know there is more that I need.

My Comments

This testimony has been given in one form or another by literally thousands of Christians in the United States, but with one exception. The others have one concluding sentence: "Since I have been baptized in the Holy Spirit, I know what it was I needed so badly." Others add, "With the baptism, I have learned how to praise God."

"Blessed be the Lord, that hath given rest unto his people ... according to all that he promised; there hath not failed one word of all his good promise" (I Kings 8:56).

A BAD CHECK

Dear Brother Carothers,

I'm learning. I'm actually praising the Lord that the check I sent you did not go through. The money was there when I wrote it, but I failed to stub the check, and in the meantime, I closed the account. The fact that you did not complain has shown me that everyone does not get upset about ordinary things like money. So, since you did not get upset, I will not either. Praise the Lord.

Let me say, too, that after reading *Prison to Praise*, I made a full commitment to Christ—that is, to become His servant in the full-time ministry. I finished college this quarter (after being a dropout for twenty years), and will enroll in Columbia Theological Seminary this summer. I praise God for your ministry and books and pray He continues to bless you richly. Thank you for sharing with me the mighty power in praise. It has opened my heart to want to give my life to God to serve Him. I knew that He wanted me to answer a call to the ministry many years ago, but I did not feel that I had anything to share with people. Now I know that the wonderful Good News of the Gospel and the joy of praise will give me many, many things to share with God's people.

My Comments

Through praise, people are learning not to get upset over their own mistakes, and this helps them not to be upset over other people's mistakes. This man's learning about praise has given the kingdom of God one more full-time minister—but even more, an enthusiastic minister! Praise the Lord!

"Then I heard the Lord asking, 'Whom shall I send as a messenger to my people? Who will go?' And I said, 'Lord, I'll go! Send *me*" (Isa. 6:8 TLB).

FROM AN AIR FORCE CHAPLAIN MAJOR

Dear Merlin,

Praise the Lord! This has been a joy day. It's so good working for the Lord. You meet such wonderful people. But people who know the Lord ought to be wonderful. Since your visit, it seems so much easier to witness to patients in the hospital, and I am so much more joyful. Thank you for teaching us the wonderful secret of praising God in everything. All of our chaplain officers seem completely different since we have started to be thankful instead of complaining and finding fault. There is much more that we need to learn about the spirit of thanksgiving, and we look forward to learning.

My Comments

I have been told of dozens of places of business that have been changed from dreary I-wish-I-didn't-have-to-go-to-work environments to an atmosphere of genuine enthusiasm for the day's work. When employers introduce the power of praise into their daily tasks, there is an overflow that blesses the entire business.

"If we are living now by the Holy Spirit's power, let us follow the Holy Spirit's leading in every part of our lives" (Gal. 5:25 TLB).

BAPTISM MADE REAL FOR BOOKSTORE MANAGER

Dear Brother Carothers,

How can one explain how much they have been blessed? Just sitting here, thinking of how I am to tell you, fills my soul so that tears just keep coming and coming.

I am the manager of a bookstore in our town, and for at least five months, I have been wanting to write to you to say how much we in the store have been blessed with your two books. I had worked here for three years, then became the manager, and I'd listen to these folks telling about the baptism in the Holy Spirit. At first, I thought they were all nuts. But I could see the joy and love they had, and finally I decided I wanted it too! I finally read *They Speak with Other Tongues*, a book I would keep in the back of the store for those fanatical folk. It did sound strange, but I wanted the love and power I saw in them.

Well, there was a great revival held at one of our leading Assembly of God churches, and I went. You bet, I did receive the Holy Spirit. What a thrill! But having a husband who believed that experience was only for the apostles, I was deflated soon after, and you will never know what mental torment I went through. The devil was really working overtime. Finally, your *Prison to Praise* came out, and believe me, as God is my witness, as soon as I read that book and began thanking God and praising Him, the doubt left me, and to this day, it has never come back. Oh, how I praise His Holy Name! I have been able to tell hundreds of people about this, and you will never know how the sale of your book increased. I had all my help read it, they got blessed, and the minute anyone enters the store, they are asked, "Have you read *Prison to Praise* and *Power in Praise*?" We just cannot keep them in stock. How I love your *Power in Praise*, too.

It is also precious to hear people tell of their new experiences in praising the Lord and thanking Him. If I had the time, I could tell you dozens of their testimonies.

I really didn't mean to write so much, but I had to tell you the whole story. I thought I was happy in becoming a Christian, which I was, but never like this. I take everything to my Savior now, with thanksgiving and praise. Oh, why aren't we taught in churches to praise the Lord? I'm telling preachers in the store, "You had better start telling your flock how to praise the Lord!"

So, how does one thank you or explain? I know you have letters every day, no doubt, explaining others' joy, too. I pray that the Lord will keep using you, keep you writing books, and I'll keep selling them and selling them for you. PRAISE GOD!

My Comments

Over and over I have heard the same testimony. When people who have received the baptism in the Holy Spirit start praising God for all things, the Holy Spirit releases faith in them to believe what God has already done for them. Regardless of what God has done for us, we can shut off His power by our grumbling doubts that He is really working all things for our good. It isn't much good to have a 200-horsepower Cadillac in the garage if we don't have faith enough to use it!

"Yet believing, ye rejoice with joy unspeakable and full of glory" (I Pet. 1:8).

AFRAID OF MY FATHER

Dear Mr. Carothers,

One week before I received your new book, *Power in Praise*, I was driving down the road, and God spoke to me so clearly. He told me to praise Him fifteen minutes every day that my father and I were just like we were in our relationship with each other. I have been afraid of my father nearly all my life. At times when he became violent, he would grab me by the hair and throw me under the bed. Now that I am married and have accepted Christ and been filled with His Spirit, I have tried many times to witness to my father and tell him about God's love. Each time he has become very violent, and I was again filled with great fear and, I suppose, anger.

In response to God's urging me to praise Him, I did it kind of halfheartedly. About the middle of the week, one afternoon as I was ironing and singing, the Holy Spirit led me to start praising my Heavenly Father for my earthly father for fifteen minutes every day, for his specific good and bad points and my good and bad points as the Holy Spirit revealed them. I was to thank God that everything was just like it was. As I was praising Him, I started shaking so bad that I couldn't even hold the iron. Talk about joy, love, and peace! God revealed to me that through my obedience to Him in praise and trust, I had released all those pent-up emotions that had built up in reference to my earthly father. Did I ever experience God's freedom! Then when I received your book, *Power in Praise*, Jesus just took me in deeper. It has really blessed me. Praise is coming to be such a living reality in my life—as close as each breath. May God bless you and your home.

My Comments

One of my great joys has been to hear and read about the many people all over the world whom God is leading into a life of praise. Many write of experiences of praising God long before they read anything that I had written or heard me speak about praising God. This reveals to me that God is opening the hearts of His people all over the world and leading them into a life of continual praise. As He spoke directly to the prophets in the Old Testament and to the disciples in the New Testament, He is now, through the Holy Spirit, ministering praise to His people all over the world.

"To give unto them ... the garment of praise for the spirit of heaviness" (Isa. 61:3).

LADY IN WHEELCHAIR NOT HEALED

A widowed mother was afflicted with a paralysis that confined her to a wheelchair. Her despair at this turn in her life brought nearly continual weeping and regret that she had ever been born. She dwelt much upon the possibility of suicide. Her three teen-age children were not only not being helped by her, but they had to continually wait upon her. Being so helpless and worthless was driving her out of her mind.

This lady was then introduced to the baptism in the Holy Spirit through reading *Prison to Praise*. She asked to be prayed for, and was gloriously filled with His Spirit. Her home became a center of praise to God. The house rang with her songs and laughter. Everyone who entered the house left with a song on their lips. The children were quickly transformed. Instead of feeling sorry for themselves for having a crippled mother, they, too, blossomed out into laughing, thankful youth.

As this mother grew in joy, she grew in praise. She thanked God for the entire event that had sentenced her to a wheelchair. She praised Him for loving her so much that He arranged her life so she could be filled with His Holy Spirit.

Friends began to pray with her for healing. Her attention centered more and more on healing. She read every book she could find on healing and corresponded with everyone she heard about who might know anything about how she could be made well by Christ. Her faith in Divine intervention grew, and she believed that soon she would be back on her feet caring for her children. They rejoiced with her and joyfully laughed about how great it would be when she could resume her place as a normal mother.

Preoccupation with healing caused this woman to praise God less and less. Her joy began to sag, and she less frequently believed that God was using the infirmity to bless her. Her prayers became more tense, urgent, and less loving. The old fears started coming back. Neighbors who had come by to laugh with her gradually appeared less and less frequently. The three children started to find excuses to be away from home. The spirit of fear took over, and the laughter was gone.

"What has happened?" she asked me. "Why can't I get back to the joy I once had? I once had more joy here in my wheelchair than I ever had in my whole life! Now I am miserable and can't find my way back."

Back? There is only one way. The spirit of praise drives out heaviness. Each of us must choose which we prefer. God knows when our faith needs to be stretched out, and He in love lets us experience what He knows is best for us. If we move back into fear, He knows that that potential lies within us, and He wants to let it be forced up where praise can go to work on it and turn our innermost being into joy.

"Let not your heart be troubled" (John 14:1).

LETTER FROM MICHIGAN

Dear Colonel Carothers,

After reading your book, I am unable to decide what I should do about two things: (1) I have members of my family who are not Christians. Should I be thankful that they are not Christians? If I am to be thankful for everything, this must be one of those things. (2) When I am sick, if I am honestly thankful for it, how can I ask the Lord to make me well?

My Comments

Many people have been unable to understand how we could praise God for something and at the same time do our part in making things as good as they can be.

It is very important that everyone understand the necessity of doing the very best that we can in every situation. God has given us abilities and talents and special gifts in order that we might use them to glorify Him. Therefore, a Christian dedicated to praising God in everything should also be dedicated to doing the very best that he can, using all the strength he has, to do everything that Christ would have done in his place. With an attitude of thanksgiving and praise, we can approach each task with joy that God has entrusted this opportunity to us, believing that He is working in us to accomplish His purpose.

Every Christian should definitely do His best to lead anyone to Christ and be thankful for the opportunity. I would never be thankful that someone wasn't saved. I would ask God to lead them to Christ and be thanking Him that He was leading them to Christ. I would not base my faith on outward evidence or things I could see, but upon faith in His Word that He would lead them to Christ.

If I had bad health, I would say, "Thank You, God, that You have permitted this condition to exist. I know that You are teaching me something wonderful through it, and now I am asking You to make me well. You also gave me the desire to be well." As I trusted God to make me well, I would continue to rejoice in whatever symptoms continued to exist. God will remove the symptoms in His own good time.

When our faith does not seem strong enough to reach out and claim God's promises, I believe that we should even thank God for our weak faith. Why? This reveals so powerfully our need of the Holy Spirit's help. We cannot believe without His help. We are forced into crying out to God for help even to believe. Paul said even our faith is a gift from God. Being forced into the humble position of recognizing our absolute dependence upon God's help is exactly what we need to be drawn to Him. One of man's greatest weaknesses is his pride in himself. Our American tradition of "doing it on our own" causes us to become so self-sufficient that we often forget our dependence upon God. We need to have confidence in our own abilities and strength, but these must continually be recognized as gifts from God.

"God has already given you everything you need ... He has given you the whole world to use . . . all of the present and all of the future. All are yours, and you belong to Christ, and Christ is God's" (I Cor. 3:21,22 TLB).

POLIO

Dear Sir,
When they first told me that I had polio, I was scared stiff. I didn't really know what it was; all I knew was

that it was something terrible. In the early days, I experienced extreme pain along with my fear and desperation. Many people came to pray for me, and my hopes would go way up, and then way down. My faith sometimes brought me joy, and sometimes I wondered if there was a God who cared about me. Everyone who talked to me seemed to think that the most important thing of all was for God to heal me. My whole attention was upon getting healed. I know it is possible for God to heal anyone, but now I know that what happens to the spirit is far more important than what happens to the body.

As it seemed unlikely that God was going to heal me, I was faced with the choice of becoming more afraid and more unhappy, or of finding some solution. Then I was given a copy of your book, *Prison to Praise*. It was like a light being turned on for me. I realized that, for me, God first wanted my praise and my thanksgiving. As I praised Him and thanked Him for my life as it was, peace started to replace my fear.

Some people would be made happy only if they heard God healed my sickness, but I want to say that He healed my spirit. I still have polio, but I'm not the same sick *person* I once was. I can laugh now, and I think I am happier than most people who come to sympathize with me.

I won't be so hypocritical as to say I don't want to be made completely well. I often think about how nice it would be to be in good health, but I have accepted the powerful force of praise into my life, and it has made a big difference in me. As I look back, I realize that I am happier now than I was before I had polio. This may sound crazy to some people, but it is true.

My Comments

The Communists say that religion is an opiate that deadens the mind to reality. We say that Christ is a power that turns reality into joy. When we are caught in circumstances that we cannot change, we have been given the glorious opportunity to let God make something good out of them.

"At last I shall be fully satisfied; I will praise you with great joy" (Ps. 63:5 TLB).

BED-WETTING

Dear Merlin,

Thank you for taking the time to write to me and for sharing your books with me. I will give you a little about my background. I am a minister and have long been very enthusiastic about evangelism. Holding classes in soul-winning in my own church and in surrounding churches has been one of my great interests. The Good News of the Gospel has been my first love for many years.

The problem we had in our home would perhaps seem comparatively minor to many people, but it was a source of pain to us, and we repeatedly cried out to God for His help. Our two sons had a severe bed-wetting problem. We took them to several doctors and tried several different remedies, but nothing seemed to help. Those parents who have not had this problem could not understand the conflict that this created in our home. My wife was under a great strain in caring for beds, and in trying to understand our sons. Any trips that we made to friends, family, or motels were continually marred by this problem.

When I read your book about praising God for problems, it was with great difficulty that I decided that our problem should be treated with thanksgiving and praise. My wife and I agreed that God had given us our children, and we should thank Him and praise Him for them as they were. Actually, we did not expect any change to take place in our sons, but we agreed that our part was to truly be thankful for them as they were.

Almost immediately, we began to notice a change in their habits. We did not tell them that we were praising God for the problem, but kept it to ourselves and God. You cannot imagine the pure delight we had as morning after morning, it became clearer and clearer to us that God was literally changing our sons as we praised Him and thanked Him for them as they were. And now after all the many cures we tried, the many prayers we made, and the many anxious hours we spent, we are experiencing the wonderful power there is in praise. I am so thankful that we were able to praise God without expecting Him to do something for us.

Thank you so much for sharing *Power in Praise* with us.

My Comments

A problem such as bed-wetting may not seem very important to the average reader, but it can be extremely nerve-racking to a family, and especially to the children. Many children's personalities are warped by the constant battle that goes on regarding this problem. As parents learn to give children over to God, He is then able to take both parents and children, and work out the problem for them. As children feel guilty when they have this problem, parents also feel guilty that they have not been able to help the child. But guilt is never the solution to any problem. Faith and trust in God solve problems, even if the outward physical manifestation is not changed. Faith brings a change in us, and the loving trust that God has given us the children and parents that are best for us. Never believe that children come to you by accident, or by the whim of nature—they are God's gift to you to meet your need.

Paul knew God was meeting his need, so when they had "thrust them into the inner prison, and made their feet fast in the stocks ... at midnight Paul and Silas prayed, and sang praises unto God: and the prisoners heard them" (Acts 16:24,25).

FROM A DISCOURAGED MINISTER

Dear Brother Carothers,

I am a minister in a different denomination from yours, but am writing to ask for your help and guidance. I have read your books and believe that it would be very wonderful to be filled with joy as you apparently are. I have so much confusion inside me that I never feel ready to preach to my people.

I am, for example, continually bothered by the problem of why we should try to do our best if God already knows what we are going to do. Part of me wants to believe that God could know what I am going to do, but still give me the the free will to make my own choices. But in my everyday experiences, I keep thinking, "Oh, what's the use?" I can't seem to generate the enthusiasm that I need to really get anything done that needs to be done.

This new emphasis on praise, instead of helping me, seems to make me even more confused about what I should be doing or feeling or believing. If you have any recommendations for suggested reading, please let me know. At one time I had a very joyful, peaceful relationship with God, but somewhere along the line, something happened. As I think about it, I believe it was in seminary that I began to lose my confidence in myself, in God, and in the work I felt called to do.

When I read the Gospels, it seems to me that everything Jesus did had been so accurately predicted that He had no choice in what He did or did not do. Then I think, "I must not have any choice either, and I will end up exactly as I am scheduled to end." If I cannot possibly change my own life, how can I expect to change anyone else's life?

Dear Brother in Christ,

I will do my best to give you my reactions to your letter.

What if there had been no Old Testament with its detailed predictions of the events in Jesus' life? I believe His life would have been lived exactly as it was. He did not live to fulfill the predictions. The predictions merely foretold God's plan in order to help us recognize Christ as His Son. The predictions also enable us to see the reality that God knows the end from the beginning.

Jesus had no control over most of the predictions concerning His life, for example, His crucifixion between two thieves, the gambling over His clothes by the guards, the thrusting of the spear through His body, and the failure of the guards to break His bones as they did of the other two men and customarily did to all who were crucified. As you know, these are only a few of the many predictions over which Jesus did not have any human control.

Your life could just as easily have been predicted by God down to the very last detail of everything that has ever happened to you. He could have had a book written about you, many years before you were born. If you had never seen or heard of the book, your life would have been exactly as it is. But a book like that would have robbed you of your personal responsibility to seek to find God's will for your life. You must learn to walk in faith, to trust Him to work out every detail to your best interest.

He could trust Jesus to walk in faith, but he couldn't trust you or me. Seeing a written account of how God is going to perfectly care for your entire life would destroy your ability to grow in faith, even as the idea of God knowing your entire life is now causing you trouble: So, you only have God's personal word that He does know everything that is ever going to happen to you. He asks you to believe this, to be filled with peace and joy, and at the same time to strive with all your might to do the very best you can. Though Jesus knew His own end from the beginning, it did not deter Him in the slightest from taking up His cross daily to follow God's plan for Him. The gruesome details of the crucifixion did not discourage Him, for He knew about the resurrection.

I believe that your greatest need now is to be filled with the Holy Spirit. The power of the Holy Spirit will pierce through your doubts, fears, and uncertainties, and the joy of God's power will be very real in your life.

My Comments

So many people say that they believe that God will work out all things for good, but the knowledge seems to be more of a head knowledge than a heart knowledge. For this reason, their lives go up and down like a roller coaster from one discouragement to another. When you believe that God loves you and that His careful guidance over every detail in your life is motivated by this great love, then you step on board another type of transportation, with a first-class seat, on an inclined plane that goes steadily, continually upward, with "joy unto joy, victory unto victory."

It is extremely important that you understand that God works everything for good in our lives because He loves us, and not simply to fulfull a promise that He made a long time ago. As we comprehend this, a power is released that helps us to believe in our heart what others believe only in their head.

"With the heart man believeth unto righteousness" (Rom. 10:10).

HEALED OF CIGARETTES

Dear Rev. Carothers,

I have read in your book *Prison to Praise* how you prayed for a man to be delivered from cigarettes, and he vomited when he tried to smoke. I desperately need your help. I have been smoking for many years. I have tried all kinds of cures, but nothing seems to help. I have been prayed for, people have tried to cast evil spirits out of me, and I have even promised God that I would never smoke again. I have taken the pills that are supposed to stop the terrible craving I have for cigarettes, but nothing has helped. I know that smoking is injuring my health and my Christian testimony. I beg you to do whatever you can to help me stop what I know is a terrible habit.

Dear Sister,

I am joyfully thanking God for the problem you have with smoking. I know that God is using it to bless you and to draw you to Him. He is using this craving that you have for cigarettes to make you realize how much you need His blessing in many other parts of your life. This problem is now resulting in God's power being made clear in your life.

I will continue to praise Him and thank Him for what has kept you down on your knees all this time, and I believe that your joy will be full. I urge you to join with me, even as you read this letter, in thanking God for all that has happened. Rejoice even for the bad habit, and believe that God is using it for your good. Praise Him for loving you enough to permit you to be so severely tempted.

Dear Rev. Carothers,

As I began to read your letter, I could not believe that you were telling me to be thankful for the terrible problem I had, but by the time I had finished your letter, I knew you must be right. I began to rejoice and to thank God for this terrible craving I have had for cigarettes, believing He was using it for my good. As I was praising the Lord and rejoicing, I felt a great weight was being lifted off my shoulders. I felt so free and so happy, but I thought, "I *can't* be healed already."

Within a few minutes, I knew that something must have happened to me, because when I thought about a cigarette, I didn't want one. A voice inside of me said I would probably want one later, but later, I still didn't want a cigarette. By the end of the day, I knew that something really tremendous had happened inside of me. After many, many years of trying to "kick the habit" myself, I found that God had done it for me.

I cannot express my gratitude. I now feel a new faith in God and in Christ. I *know* that I am a Christian. I thought I knew before, but there was always a doubt of some kind inside of me. I still have other problems, but it is thrilling to believe that God will use even my problems to help me. I am filled with thanksgiving and praise for everything!

My Comments

Since I prayed years ago for a soldier to "never again smoke another cigarette," I have seldom been led to ask God to deliver people instantly from smoking. I have perceived that one bad habit would frequently be replaced with another—until the individual has learned to put his own spirit above his physical desires. It takes only a second for Jesus to make people well, but it may take much longer for people to realize how much they need His help.

If the kind of praying you have been used to has left you with nothing but discouragement, try the prayer of praise and thanksgiving! If you experience less than instantaneous deliverance, do not say, "Well, that doesn't work either." Your very declaration would be evidence that you had not really been thankful for your situation exactly as it is and believed that God was using it. Whatever the results, your only alternative on the pathway to victory is to "rejoice always," not with lip service alone, but with pure praise to God in your heart for His faithful ministry to your *every need*! If God permits you to be tempted, He has to have some good reason!

"God is faithful, who will not suffer you to be tempted above that ye are able; but will with the temptation also make a way to escape that ye may be able to bear it" (I Cor. 10:13).

BAD HABITS AND CHURCH

Dear Rev. Carothers,

I recently finished your book, *Prison to Praise*, and I thank God for providing it to me. As soon as I finished it, I knelt down and accepted Christ. I now have the first real joy and peace I have ever known. I would never have read your book if my wife had not left me. Her leaving caused me to want to reach out for help from God. She had asked me to read your book, and so I did. Since this wonderful change has come into my life, I am now able to thank God that my wife and two children have left me. But I am also believing that she will come back, and am trusting God to bring her.

My wife and I have been married for five years and six months. We have had some pretty hard times. We weren't right with the Lord. We have two beautiful children, one boy and one girl, and they were being affected by our fussing and fighting all the time. So one week, when I got back from a trip, I found her and the children gone.

I just want to praise and thank God for this because of all the good that has come out of it. I now know God and believe He is going to help me. I pray that I might be able to show my wife real joy in serving the Lord. Please pray for my wife, that she, too, will trust the Lord and will find her way back to Him.

My wife is having a real battle with her smoking, and she is afraid and ashamed to face the people in the church.

Please pray for me that I might grow in faith, and keep praising God for all the good that has come from my wife's leaving. I now know that it is His will for us to be united.

My Comments

God always uses every situation to work out some good. His power is especially released as we learn to thank Him and to trust Him. A real problem is revealed in this letter regarding the wife and her relationship to her church. She had evidently been trained to believe that if she was guilty of smoking, she could not also be a Christian. This teaching drove her to abandon her church and her faith because she could not give up her bad habit. There has to be something very wrong when people guilty of a bad habit are afraid to go to church. When any church over-emphasizes the harm in smoking, they probably want to help the people. But I have seen much eternal harm done to men and women when they turn away from God because they cannot live up to standards that men have given to them. It is right to teach against bad habits, but this teaching becomes wrong if it is not clearly emphasized that faith in Christ gives us eternal life. His power in us will enable us to give up all habits that are harmful as we trust in Him. With this understanding, everyone should be able to gather together with the assurance that God understands each of their weaknesses. As they share together and love one another, He will help them to grow in strength and grace.

"Thanks be unto God, which always causeth us to triumph in Christ" (II Cor. 2:14).

LUST

Dear Chaplain Carothers,
I have a terrible thing inside of me. Since you spent many years with men, you may be able to advise me. I keep having lust in my heart for women other than my

wife. I know Jesus said this made me guilty of adultery, and I keep trying to stop. I even tell God I will never do it again, but it keeps coming back, even though I know it is wrong. I enjoy these thoughts while I am having them. At the time, it gives me great pleasure, but then the guilt comes, and I know I have done wrong. One part of me says, "God made you like you are, so how could He blame you?" The other part says, "He wants to change you so you will be more like Christ."

Please give me any advice you can, and please ask God to help me do whatever He wants me to do. I cannot change myself.

Dear Brother,

Thank you for your very frank request for help. God will always honor such honesty. There is one part of your problem that you have not yet understood. You do indeed receive pleasure from impure thoughts, but it is a mere imitation of the pleasure God wants to give you. Satan knows this, so he is making a mighty effort to rob you of what God wants you to have. Yes, God gave you a natural desire for women, but Satan has corrupted both the desire and the pleasure. When the Holy Spirit helps you to let Him control the desire, you will experience a new kind of pleasure that will make the old seem as nothing! When you can look at a beautiful woman with praise and thanksgiving to God for making such a lovely creation, His joy will fill your heart. He will be receiving your praise, and you will be receiving His joy.

Never be discouraged. More Christian men than you may realize are fighting this same problem. Believe now that Jesus gives you pure thoughts. When Satan tries to ride into you on the same old mental tracks, put up your "stop" sign, start praising God for His creation, and see what happens. You may even weep with the joy He gives!

"The peace of God, which passeth all understanding, shall keep your hearts and minds through Christ Jesus" (Phil. 4:7).

HUSBAND COMES HOME

Dear Reverend Carothers,

I had been under a great burden for nearly two years. My husband was living with another woman, and I had not heard from him in eighty-two days. This Friday morning I vowed I had to get needed help, and I planned to leave for Fort Benning, Georgia, to see you. The Lord checked me, and I was led to telephone to see if by chance you were on vacation. After many calls, I found you had retired and were in a different state. I reached your residence and left a message for you to call me. Many hours later, you called and I told you I was impressed with the tape of the message you delivered in El Paso, Texas, in 1970, at the Full Gospel Business Men's meeting, and with your book, *Prison to Praise*. I told you my need, and you said you would pray with me over the telephone.

After our talk and your prayer, I felt nothing. I seemed so empty, and the enemy even made me doubt and say, "Did I just spend money for nothing?" That was how I felt—but as I crossed the kitchen and entered the living room, still numb, I sat down and leaned my head back and all at once I was laughing and laughing out loud. I said, "Thank You, Lord!"

Within hours my husband came home. But he came home to a different woman. Instead of nagging and fussing, I was filled with a new laugh. This laugh is with me now in every part of my life. I can easily thank God for leading me through deep waters.

My Comments

Often God has to change us before He can change our circumstances. Most people want Him to change others rather than themselves! The "terrible sins" others are involved in are used as a blindfold to cover up the need for change in our own lives.

"To give unto them ... the garment of praise for the spirit of heaviness" (Isa. 61:3).

REJECTED

Dear Sir,

My father was quite open in his hatred for me. Mother told me over and over again how much she loved me. I grew up depending on her love. However, in my early teens, she turned on me one day and said, "I've only pretended to love you. No one could love you the way you are."

My world was shattered, and I determined never to need anyone again. I became totally self-sufficient and dedicated myself to doing everything better than anyone else. When I had an unusually good job and was earning good money, I met a handsome man who seemed to be all I had ever dreamed of. He was able to completely open my heart, and I was able to love and receive love. My life centered in this man for many months. Then one day he called me from a distant town and said, "I have something to tell you that you are not going to like. I've just gotten married!"

The world stopped for me. Nothing was worth living for. It was evident to me that there must be something terribly wrong with me. Was I unlovable or stupid? I didn't know which.

From this experience, I fell into a psychiatrist's office. He comforted me week after week, until I became totally dependent upon him. This went on until it dawned on me, "This man wants me to be dependent on him. He either needs someone to depend on him or he wants the thousands of dollars that I have paid him." The realization of this knocked another prop out from under me, and that brings you up to date in my sad story. There is only one more thing to tell.

A friend gave me a copy of your book, *Prison to Praise*. As I read it, I decided, "This is the only hope I have. I can either kill myself, or get to the writer of that book and ask him to pray for me."

Can you do anything for me?

Dear Friend,

No, I cannot, but I can direct you to Someone who can. His fees are rather high. He wants your love, because He loves you. He has permitted every trace of self-sufficiency to be drained out of you. You are now completely dependent upon Him, and you know it. It has been painful to you, I know, but God has actually been blessing you in all of this. You feel unloved, and you believe it is because of something wrong in you.

God tells me to tell you He loves you as you are. Don't try to change yourself. Thank Him that you are exactly as you are, have had your exact experiences, and are now in the exact place you are. You have been injured by others, but don't blame yourself for that. If your parents had broken your arm, you wouldn't blame yourself for that, would you? They hurt your ability to give and receive love, and this is no more your fault than a broken arm would be. Believe that God loves you, and I promise you a powerful change in your life. My prayers will be with you, and Jesus is beside you as you read this.

Dear Sir,

I had a feeling you would tell me something like you did, but I had no idea of how it would hit me. I put your letter on a chair and put my head on top of it and promptly covered it in an ocean of tears. These were the first tears of joy I had cried in a long while. What happened to me had to be caused by more than just the words in your letter. As I read, I *knew* God loved me. I knew His love would only grow stronger. As I praised Him for *me* as I am, I actually liked me.

There are still fears in my mind, but the big one is gone, and I know I am getting well. The more I thank God for the things that have happened, the less fear I have about the future.

My Comments

Many people rest in self-confidence only because they have never had all the props knocked out from under them. They have weathered many storms and overcome many difficult problems. Their self-confidence grows, and it seems as if they will make it all their lives without God. Then God in His wonderful goodness reaches out and withdraws everything that they trusted in or believed in. Love for others and even for self is gone. What hope is left? When every avenue of escape is investigated and nothing leads out of the despair, the helpless soul reaches out to God. If we are there to tell them God loves them as they are, His love meets every need they have. If we tell them, "You have to do this, or that, or something else, before God will completely accept you," they are not helped. These creatures have often done all they can do, are exhausted, and are ready to fall into the arms of God.

"Thy lovingkindness is better than life, my lips shall praise thee. Thus will I bless thee while I live: I will lift up my hands in thy name" (Ps. 63:3,4).

NOT GOOD ENOUGH

Dear Mr. Carothers,

Your first book, *Prison to Praise*, set me on fire, but I thought I wasn't good enough to receive the baptism in the Holy Spirit. Your second book, *Power in Praise*, helped me to realize that nobody is good enough. The baptism is free just like salvation. Now I have received the baptism, and oh, the joy and love I received with it!

My Comments

When anyone tells me they are not good enough to receive the baptism in the Holy Spirit, I always respond joyfully, "If you feel that way, you are ready to receive!" Anyone who feels good enough to receive the baptism could not possible receive it!

Others say, "I would like to receive, but I do not understand it." To them, I also respond in joy, "If you realize that you don't understand it, you are ready to receive!"

The baptism in the Holy Spirit is designed in such a way that little children and people with the simple faith of a little child can receive it.

———————

"Anyone who humbles himself as this little child, is the greatest in the Kingdom of Heaven" (Matt. 18:4 TLB).

THANKFUL FOR EVIL PEOPLE?

Dear Sir,

If I am supposed to thank God for everything, does that mean I should thank Him for the terribly evil people who are around me and probably in many parts of the world? I don't want to be thankful for them. I want them to be changed.

My Comments

If evil people are to be changed, He has to do it. If He wants to use our thanksgiving to do it, should we complain? "The Lord hath made all things for himself: Yea, even the wicked for the day of evil" (Prov. 16:4). God surely must know what He is doing better than I do. He is now in the process of using many wrong things in my past to help others. I must believe that He can use all evil if we trust Him.

"The Son of man shall come in the glory of his Father with his angels; and then he shall reward every man according to his works" (Matt. 16:27).

NEED FOR LOVE

Dear Rev. Carothers,

My husband is very strong-willed, talented, verbal, good, keen, authoritative, has very few problems, can handle anything, expects perfection in everyone, knows best about everything, and thinks he is open-minded. After reading *Prison to Praise*, I knew that my task in life was to learn to be thankful for him exactly as he is. At first I couldn't do it. No matter how hard I tried, I failed. I was always under a feeling of condemnation that I couldn't do what I was supposed to do. I felt bitterness, resentment, fear, doubt, anxiety, and many unpleasant emotions.

But Jesus is Lord, and He had mercy on me. He began to strengthen my faith and reassure me of how much He loved me. How difficult it had been for me to receive that love. I learned that if I, through faith, could accept my husband as he was, then I, through faith, could accept myself as I was. Somehow this released a whole new understanding to me, and great peace came into my life. Thank you for sharing with me that God loves me just as I am, and wants me to love others just as they are.

My Comments

Some people are so "very good" that they are difficult to live with. Other people are so "very bad" that they are difficult to live with. Through our praise, God will teach us something new by using every person that comes in our lives. Some of them may irritate us and drive us up the wall, but they have a mission in our lives, and God will use them to work out some greater purpose in our lives.

———————

"For of him, and through him, and to him, are all things: to whom be glory for ever" (Rom. 11:36).

THEFT

Dear Rev. Carothers,

Thank you for writing *Prison to Praise*. I would like to tell you of an experience I had that was to me extremely unusual.

I was able to get a new tape deck for my car. You may know that young people consider this a wonderful thing to have. After I had gotten it working fine and was enjoying beautiful music, I came out to my car one morning and found the tape player gone. Not only this, but they had messed up the whole dashboard in taking it out.

I knew that the devil was going to pounce on me right away, because I had read your book. So I decided to get the jump on him first, and I started saying, "Thank You, Lord, for what has happened." To my amazement, I started feeling very happy. Joy started running around inside of me. I actually felt the best I had for many weeks. Now I am beginning to understand a little bit about what you meant when you said there was real joy in praising God for everything. I expect to keep learning, and I thank God for what you have shared with me.

My Comments

Praise God.

"But I rejoiced in the Lord greatly ... for I have learned ... to be content" (Phil. 4:10,11).

TIC DOULOUREUX

Dear Rev. Carothers,

I've suffered a great deal from Tic Douloureux.* I feel that the Lord paid me a great compliment in believing I could suffer so much and yet continue to praise Him. It's been said that this disease causes one of the most terrible pains known to man. May God bless you as you serve Him and continue to teach others the wonderful power there is in praising God for everything. I know that praising Him looses one of the most powerful forces in the world.

My Comments

This letter was written with a very evidently pain-filled hand. I have checked with medical authorities, and indeed, this particular affliction is one of the most painful known to man. It is a disease of the nerves, so excruciating that sometimes surgery has to be performed to completely sever the nerves.

I recommend that whatever pain you may be having, you remember this child of God, who has discovered a wonderful secret. She has learned that when God permits any kind of suffering, it is because of His love for us rather than disinterest in our needs. Eternity will provide ample opportunity for God to reward our faith and trust in Him. If you will now believe God loves you too much to always respond to your every desire, you will then become more free to love Him and to experience His love overflowing in your heart.

It is an absolute reality that often people who have experienced severe pain love God more than most other people do.

There are people who lose faith in God because of their pain, but this does not change the positive reality that when we trust God, He uses even pain to draw us closer to Him. There is an old saying that applies to this: "The same sun hardens the clay, and melts the ice."

"And we know that all things work together for good to them that love God, to them who are called according to his purpose" (Rom. 8:28).

*A kind of facial neuralgia.

ASHAMED

Dear Sir,

I now realize how completely I have wasted most of my life on selfish, worthless things. Christ has come into my heart, and I want to do what I can to make up for all the wasted time. Do you have any suggestions as to what I could do? Making money was part of my old life, and I now have more than enough to help others, but there are so many needy people in the world that I couldn't help them all. If you have any special recommendations, I would be pleased to hear from you. After reading your books, I believe you have a very special communication line with God and could hear what He wants me to do.

Dear Christian,

First, I ask you one thing: Is Christ ashamed of you? Certainly not. He is proud of you. You are now His brother, and He proudly presents you to the Father. Paul exhorts you to have the mind of Christ in all things. If He is not ashamed of you or your past, you should not be either. God used your past to help you find Christ, didn't He? Shame robs you of the joy Jesus wants you to have in Him! Don't boast of your past, but don't continually reproach yourself or try to find ways to "make up for it." You can't do it. Jesus has already done it for you. You can't "make up for it" any more than you can change it.

God wants you to serve Him because you love Him and want to serve Him—not to try to pay Him something you think you owe Him. If you really want to serve God, then believe more and more that Jesus takes care of all the past and that He is now taking everything in your past and working it out for something good. He receives all the credit—you get nothing but the benefits. With love for Him, now ask the Holy Spirit to let you do something to make your life more meaningful. Lay up treasures in heaven.

———————

"Bless the Lord, O my soul, and forget not all his benefits: Who forgiveth all thine iniquities" (Ps. 103:2,3).

FINANCIAL PROBLEMS

Dear Rev. Carothers,

I live in and own a home that is now costing me ten times more in taxes than it did when I first moved here. I have two offers to purchase this property and would receive a handsome profit if I sold. In addition, I have the opportunity to purchase another piece of property which is not as nice but can easily be repaired and made into something very beautiful.

And now, the big decision. Should we leave something we know and love and move to something not as nice, or should we stay and trust our financial needs will be met?

I had asked for God's help and guidance in what to do, but kept going round and round, unable to make up my mind. I stayed in a turmoil about it.

Then I read, "Keep your eyes on Christ and keep

praising Him." This is what I have been doing lately, and what a difference it has made! It is amazing what happens when we trust. Some people say they are waiting on the Lord to tell them what to do. I am so dumb that I need to be hit on the head with a hammer! Now I believe that in some way He will help me to know what decision to make. In the meantime, I have experienced an overwhelming, amazing peace.

My Comments

There are many people who have not had the experience of "hearing from God," but this in no way detracts from the power there is in trusting in Him. If you do not receive any specific guidance from God, this is your great opportunity to trust Him and believe that even though you seem to be on your own, you are never alone. His Son is fulfilling His promise to be with you always even unto the end of the world.

"Ye, always having all sufficiency in all things" (II Cor. 9:8).

A NEW MINISTER

Dear Merlin,

Your two books were given to me last week by a fellow Methodist minister. I have found them of inestimable worth in my recent venture of faith. As a result of reading them, my entire outlook on God's power has been changed. Of course, I always knew that God was all powerful, but I doubted His intervention in this world. Since I have read your works, I see on every hand, evidence of the Holy Spirit working. I guess I am what you called "turned on." I feel as if I am just beginning a wonderful new adventure, and I want to share this glorious feeling with everyone. I find myself praising God and thanking Him all day long, and the more I thank Him, the more excited I become about the privilege of being a minister of the Gospel.

Tonight I had the opportunity to preach at a church of another denomination in our community. I felt new power as I ministered. I was so overflowing with joy and praise that it seemed to me that it was flowing out of me and going to everyone in the congregation. There were about two hundred people present at the service, and at the close I invited everyone who wanted to give their life over to God to serve Him completely, to come forward and stand with me at the altar. At least 85 percent of the people present came forward. In spite of many invitations that the pastor himself had given in the church, no one had ever come to the altar. I know now that God honored my praise of Him, and He reached out and touched the other people. I thank Him for the opportunity to learn just a little about the full power there is in praise.

My Comments

Many churches are being made alive as they learn together the glorious secret of praising God. Many prayer groups and Bible studies are being filled with a new song of laughter and joy as they join together in praise and thanksgiving, in worshiping God, rather than continually repeating old well-worn prayers and exhortations for God to change things that they've been praying to be changed for many years, without seeing any changes come. Now they are praising God, and new power is flowing. God is blessing in unusual ways. People are learning to actually enjoy going to church as they discover that the Holy Spirit is here in the world to make worshiping God the most enjoyable experience in our life. If you have found going to church dull, drab, or boring, I recommend that you step into a life of praise. Urge those around you to rejoice together, and see for yourself the wonderful power there is in praising God.

"Thou shalt rejoice in the Lord, and thou shalt glory in the Holy One of Israel" (Isa. 41:16).

FROM A COLONEL IN THE UNITED STATES ARMY

Dear Chaplain Carothers,

Thank you for having us on your mailing list. The Lord is really revealing Himself in this year's class at the Command and General Staff College, and praise the Lord, He is moving in unusual ways.

We are giving Christian books to as many Army officers here as we can get to read them. We are finding more opportunities to give your book than any others. So many people here at Fort Leavenworth are open to your message on praise. Now another book, too—that's almost too good!

Maybe this will or won't sound strange to you, but I thought Jesus couldn't possibly just want me to praise, so I stayed with the nitty-gritty, too, but really got dragged down in it, and praise was difficult. I began to get "religious," too, and then—ugh! But Jesus really means for us to glorify Him. Amazing, but it is so good to know He does. A real relief! Praising God is so much better than just being afraid of Him. Thank you for opening my heart to His wonderful love. I have been a Christian for many years, but now, for the first time, I am excited about the joy of serving Christ. Your ministry on praise has changed my whole life, and I am seeing other lives change continually.

My Comments

Men who have been in the Army for several years have usually seen life at its very worst. When they learn to praise God for everything, they are including many of the most painful experiences man has ever known. This kind of praise is more effective than the "splinter in the finger" type. Could you be thankful for a splinter?

———————

"Praise our God, all ye his servants, and ye that fear him, both small and great" (Rev. 19:5).

WHAT IS GOOD?

Dear Rev. Carothers,

Since I read your books, there are so many things that I can see work out for good as I praise Him and trust Him. My life is so much more joyful than it used to be, but I still have the problem of not knowing which things God is now using for good. I'm not always able to determine whether what He is doing now is good, or whether He is going to work something out of it that will be good later. I find myself repeatedly trying to determine what is and what is not good.

Can you give me any guidelines or understanding as to how I can know when something is good now, and when I should think of it as becoming good later?

My Comments

How can God possibly work *this* for good? Let's see: He could do this, if that happened. Change this and make it more like that. Or if He sees *that* is going to happen later, He can change this to fit that. On and on speculation can go, to try to figure out what God may or may not do. This kind of speculation may temporarily satisfy you and get you to accept some unpleasant situation while you wait for God to change it to do something more suitable to your desires.

"How do you get God to change so many things for you?" I am often asked. I do not "get Him to change things," for it is not the "things" that I center my attention on. It is natural to want *things* to be changed, but it is supernatural power that God uses, to change *our nature*, rather than "things."

So, how do you get things changed that are painful, harmful, or damaging? The answer is found in II Cor. 4:18. "While we look not at the things which are seen, but at the things which are not seen: for the things which are seen are temporal; but the things which are not seen are eternal." There it is. Get your eyes on the eternal. God has placed you here on this earth for an eternal reason. He uses the temporal to prepare us for the eternal. "Our light affliction, which is but a moment, worketh for us a far more exceeding and eternal weight of glory" (II Cor. 4:17).

Through experience, I have learned that when we get our eyes off that difficult situation and focus them on God, we no longer need the affliction! It has already completed its purpose, the purpose being to get our eyes away from anything temporal and on the eternal. In heaven there will only be the eternal, and we will have no opportunity to place our faith in Jesus to be victorious over the earthly. It pleases God to see His people believe that Christ is victorious in all things. He permits Satan to work all kinds of mischief in order that we may be His instruments to prove that Jesus never fails.

Let it become second nature to you. No matter what happens, don't try to figure out what good may or may not come out of painful things. Give it quickly over to God and believe that He is working it out through His Son. No matter how frequently Satan brings it back to your mind, give it right over to God. Your spiritual muscles will grow while you have your eyes on God's eternal plan. You will frequently be made aware that without any agonizing prayers on your part, He has, on His own initiative, done what your natural being wanted all the time.

Does all this sound too complicated to you? Really, it is complicated. Anything easy to understand would be understood by anyone who didn't strive to understand. Jesus taught you to strive. If you want to move forward in your spiritual life, you have to do considerably more than sleep through church services! Jesus challenged us! There is more to learn than we can possibly learn in this lifetime. How do we move mountains by faith, raise the dead, transport our bodies from one place to another, supply bread to feed thousands? Ephesians 3:20 says, "Now unto him that is able to do exceeding abundantly above all that we ask or think, according to the power that worketh in us." How do you get that power? That question is answered correctly in II Cor. 12:9: "Most gladly therefore will I rather glory in my infirmities, that the power of Christ may rest upon me!" Glory (find joy) in every situation, because you know it is part of God's eternal plan. He hasn't asked you to close your eyes to reality! Reality is that God uses all things for your good. Reality is that when you believe this, the power of Christ is released in your life.

"I ... ask the God of our Lord Jesus Christ, the glorious Father, to give you the Spirit, who will make you wise and reveal God to you, so that you will know him. I ask that your minds may be opened to see his light, so that you will know what is the hope to which he has called you ... " (Eph. 16-18 TEV).

DEAF

Dear Mr. Carothers,

My mother bought your book, *Prison to Praise*, in a Bible bookstore a few weeks ago. I kept reading it for three days.

I am a Christian, twenty-nine years old. My mother had German measles before I was born, and I was born nearly deaf. I am able to hear very little.

I graduated from high school and later from a business college. I took an examination for an IBM key-punch operator in the county civil-service examination and passed, but I have not been able to get a job yet.

God has not healed my hearing, but now I keep my eyes on Him who is my Source of supply, Friend, Helper, Savior, and Lord of every day and night.

May God touch your heart and speak to you. Pray for me that God will heal me completely at any moment and also that God will meet all my needs and send all kinds of miracles into my life.

Please write me a letter soon.

My Comments

There are many people who are longing for a miracle in their life who do not realize that miracles are already taking place in their life. The greatest miracle of all miracles is that a simple human creature should be transformed by the love of God into His child. In this case, God has used the infirmity of a young man to lead him into a very evident loving relationship with God. If he had been born with normal hearing, he might have gone the way of a great many young men and never have known Christ as his Savior.

The promise is, "My God shall supply all your need according to his riches in glory by Christ Jesus" (Phil.

4:19). What you now have is what you have needed. If it has accomplished its purpose it can pass away.

"But when that which is perfect is come, then that which is in part shall be done away" (I Cor. 13:10).

INFIDELITY

Dear Rev. Carothers:

Many years ago when I was very young, I was unfaithful to my husband. Several years ago I told my husband what I had done, and it seemed as if a wall came between us. He has tried to forgive me, but often when he looks at me I feel he is wishing that he had a wife who had never been touched by another man.

Your books tell me to be thankful for all things. I do not see how I can be thankful for what happened to me. The rest of my life was so unmarked by sin, and I could have been a better wife and had a life filled with joy if this one terrible thing had not happened to me. How could I honestly be thankful for it? I need to do something, for I am now unable to do anything for the Lord because of this feeling of guilt. If you can help me, please do so.

Dear Sister,

To be thankful for any sin we have committed does no good unless we couple it with God's forgiveness. Whenever you think of your sin, begin to praise God that He has forgiven you. This will release a powerful force. You will learn to appreciate the marvelous grace of God more than ever before. It is natural to want to have always been a pure flower for everyone to admire and respect, but if you were pure, you would not have needed Christ! God in His goodness to you permitted you to have an experience that has revealed to you how much you need His forgiveness! You needed His forgiveness all the time, but because of this experience, you are better able to see how much you needed it.

If you had never committed that sin, the potential was still there. You could have lived what you thought was a perfectly good life and have never been aware of what lurked within you.

There are people all around you who feel too depraved and unworthy ever to try to talk to God. You are now able to sense a little of what they feel. You can reach out and help them to come to Christ. Surely you can be glad that God has helped you to become more understanding of others! You have eternal life, but there are many around you who do not. God will use all of your experiences to help you and others if you will be thankful for all these things.

Your husband is guilty of his own sins. His are as great or greater than your own. Forget what you have done, if possible, but if not, then continue to praise the Lord for His forgiveness. Satan cannot stand to remain in that kind of atmosphere. He will go off and leave you "for a season." He may come back later to check you out and see if you are open again to discouragement. When he tempted you to sin, he was also interested in gaining an opportunity to torment you whenever he wanted to. When he sees you rejoicing in God's grace and forgiveness, he will go off and find someone else to torment.

"And when the devil had ended all the temptation, he departed from him for a season" (Luke 4:13).

PRAISE BRINGS BAPTISM

Dear Sir,

In your book, *Prison to Praise*, you indicate that we cannot really learn to praise God without the help of the Holy Spirit. I would like to share with you something further that I have learned. I wrote to you a few months ago asking you to pray for me that I might receive the baptism in the Holy Spirit. You wrote back and urged me to begin praising God for the problems that I mentioned, and then God would then begin to help me in a new way.

I really had been wanting the baptism in the Holy Spirit. I had studied the Bible, and was convinced that it was for me. I had gone to several groups and asked for prayer, but I didn't seem to be able to get through my head what it was they were trying to tell me. My heart was very hungry for more of Jesus, but I didn't seem to be able to find Him. When I took your advice and began thanking God for all my problems, I began to experience a new kind of fellowship with Christ. His words began to mean more to me than ever before. My faith began to increase, and I believed that God would fill me with His Spirit. The more I thanked God, the stronger my faith became. And so, through praising God, the Holy Spirit came into my life in a new way. I am thankful that praise has meant so much in my life.

My Comments

Yes, it is true, that as the Holy Spirit helps us to praise God, praising God will also help us to be filled with His Spirit. Since God, "inhabitest the praises of [His people]" (Ps. 22:3), when we praise God, we open the door for His Holy Spirit to move into our lives in a new dimension. The reverse is likewise true. When we fail to praise God and are filled with fear, uncertainty, and doubt, our hearts are closed to the moving of the Holy Spirit.

"Be filled with the Spirit ... giving thanks always for all things unto God and the Father in the name of our Lord Jesus Christ" (Eph. 5:18,20).

FROM A CELL

Dear Rev. Carothers,

I received your letter. I can't thank you enough for writing. When I opened your letter, I cried like a baby. This is something I have not done for a long time.

I would like to tell you something that happened to me in the past week. The woman I was living with came to see me. She said, "I have something to tell you. I have gotten married again. We are finished." Needless to say, I love this woman very much. When I got back to my cell that night, I was very upset. Then I remembered something you said in your book. I got down on my knees and said, "Thank You, Lord." I prayed. When I was finished, I no longer thought the future was nil for me. I felt at peace. I know now there is a future for me, but only with the help of our Savior. Through Him, I know I have a chance. You don't know what it means to me, Sir, to know it's not too late.

God bless you, Rev. Carothers. You just don't know how thankful I am to you for showing me the way.

My Comments

There is no such thing as it being too late for God to bring joy and peace into our lives. We may have had to suffer for our mistakes in the past, but He has promised to fill our hearts with joy. He may not change your situation, but He will fill you with that new wine that will cause you to give thanks for all things.

"O wretched man that I am! Who shall deliver me from the body of this death? I thank God through Jesus Christ our Lord" (Rom. 7:24,25).

NO SELF-CONFIDENCE

Dear Sir,

No matter what I do, something goes wrong. I'm losing all my self-confidence. I used to believe I had the world by the tail and could do anything I wanted to do. I accepted Christ as my Savior and expected a wonderful future for myself and family. Now I am so discouraged. I don't believe I can even keep on trying. Do you know anyone in this area who could help me?

Dear Friend,

Let it not be said of you, "In this thing ye did not believe the Lord your God" (Deut. 1:32). You did not come into the situation by accident! It is the very place God meant for you to be. Did you ever ask God to make you humble? He has placed you in a school where you are learning. Instead of being discouraged, give your problem to Christ. He knows the solution: "This thing is too heavy for thee; thou art not able to perform it thyself alone" (Exod. 18:18).

I contacted a friend who will come to see you soon. But remember, he is not your answer. Jesus is.

"I am with you; that is all you need. My power shows up best in weak people. Now I am glad to boast about how weak I am; I am glad to be a living demonstration of Christ's power, instead of showing off my own power and abilities" (II Cor. 12:9 TLB).

AN ASTRONAUT IS BURIED

Dear Rev. Carothers,

Eight years ago my brother was scheduled to make a trip to the moon as one of our country's astronauts. As he was landing after a routine flight, near the astronaut training base at Houston, the canopy flew off his T-38 jet trainer. A few minutes later he lay dead near the plane's wreckage. His parachute had only partially opened. An investigation revealed that a goose may have smashed through the canopy, and caused the accident. The pain of this loss had not subsided over the years, and I suffered repeatedly the anguish caused by losing my kid brother.

When you taught me to praise God for everything, I was able to accept this loss and receive God's healing love. Thank you for sharing Christ's love with me.

My Comments

The loss of a loved one brings pain. This pain can go on and on indefinitely unless a person learns to believe that God in His love has His own perfect plan for us and our loved ones. When we give them over to Him, the pain will leave and be replaced by His peace. Jesus said, "Bring your burdens to me, and leave them there." This includes all the burdens of life. If we trust Him, we are supposed to leave our problems with Him and let Him take care of them. If we don't trust Him, we are tempted to turn back and pick them up again. As Christians, we know that God wants us to be different from others.

"Gather us from among the heathen, to give thanks unto thy holy name, and to triumph in thy praise" (Ps. 106:47).

TEETH-GRITTING

Dear Merlin:

I've just finished your books, *Prison to Praise* and *Power in Praise*. Thank you. Thank you. Thank you.

I've always thought myself a Christian (being born and raised a Catholic), but I've always had difficulty accepting the various things that have happened in my life. I've gritted my teeth and wondered many times, "Why?" It seemed so petty or meaningless. Frankly, I can't find the right words now. Before I read you books, I could have described my life in detail. I've been rereading your books, and each time I find some deeper meaning. My life hasn't changed—no dramatic doorbells ringing with a lost love returning, or anything like that. But now I can joyfully accept the heavy traffic, the spilled coffee, the woman fellow-worker who works with her mouth more than her work, my lost son, the empty house.

Now, I know *why*, and can thank God properly and love Him. I feel as though the heavy burdens have been lifted. I'm trying to share my new joy with my sisters and brothers as I encounter them. I can't explain as beautifully and concisely as you do, so from all of us—THANKS!

My Comments

When you don't know any better method, I guess gritting your teeth would have to do. But why be satisfied with poverty of spirit when God has offered us fullness of joy?

"These things have I spoken unto you ... that your joy might be full" (John 15:11).

I WAS MAD

Dear Rev. Carothers,

When my wife came home and said she had received the baptism in the Holy Spirit and had spoken in tongues, I was mad, real mad. Not at her, but at those stupid people who had convinced her of something I knew to be of the devil.

We had attended church and taken part in all its activities all of our lives. My parents were born-again Christians, and I had heard them talking several times about the "Holy Roller tongues-speakers." When I told them what had happened to my wife, I could see they were really upset. They called our minister, and he agreed to have the whole church pray for my wife to be saved from this terrible experience.

My wife agreed to go with me to talk to the preacher if I would read a book called *Prison to Praise*. I agreed. By the time I finished reading your book, I was thoroughly confused. If God had done the things that you claimed, then speaking in tongues couldn't be of the devil.

None of the miracles you wrote about had ever happened in our church. My anger subsided, and I asked my wife to pray with me so I would know what to do. Then it happened! I was filled with the Holy Spirit, too!

My life has been completely changed. I once went to church because I knew it was the thing I ought to do. There certainly was no joy there, but I did get a certain amount of peace from doing what I thought was good. Now I enjoy worshiping God! We go to prayer groups that last until midnight, and I'm never ready to leave. At work and at home I feel a continual sense of Christ's presence with me. I thank God for letting me experience the power Jesus promises to His disciples. I've led several people to Christ since He baptized me, and I had never led one person to Him before that.

My Comments

Being satisfied with what always has been, may be all right for the believer himself, but it does not help the man who will never be a believer until someone shares with him the Good News of the Gospel. Some Christians who have not received the baptism in the Holy Spirit do witness for Christ, but when they receive His power they become many times more effective witnesses. There are now hundreds of thousands of testimonies to this. If the baptism in the Holy Spirit sets people's hearts aflame to tell others about Jesus, could it be wrong? If it leads men to Christ, it is easy to see why Satan is so afraid of it!

"Ye shall receive power after that the Holy Ghost is come upon you: and ye shall be witnesses unto me" (Acts 1:8).

WIFE GONE

Dear Brother Carothers,
My wife and I have been married for five years and six months, and in this time I have treated her pretty bad. I guess we were both like two children holding onto our mothers. But a month ago she took our two children and left me and filed for divorce.
I thank God that she left, because if it were not for this, I would still be on my way to hell. But I believe that this is God's way of giving us that Christian home we both wanted and prayed for for so long.

My Comments

Being part of a home that is filled with agony is probably one of the most difficult experiences any of us will ever have. The sheer weight of the burden has caused many people to completely give up. But God has promised to use even this tragedy to help us if we will trust Him. It boils down to the absolute conclusion that we should be filled with peace regardless of what is going on around us. Why? Because God has promised to use it for our good.

When you have done the best that you know how to do, don't let Satan saddle you with remorse. Remember that God can change any situation in a split second. He can make people change their attitudes, minds, thinking, or anything He wants to do. There is nothing He cannot do. His authority is final and absolute. He can wield all this power in love because His final goal is our eternal happiness. He overlooks our temporal desires, no matter how strong they are, because He knows our future and is determined to help us grow. Do you believe He is able to do anything? If so, your opportunity to prove it is in your situation. He has permitted you to be there at this moment, for His own good reason.

Remember the vineyard owner. He hired some men at the crack of dawn and others near the end of the day. He paid them all the same. Then the grumbling began. Jesus said the owner could do exactly as he wanted because he was being fair to everyone. God can do as He wants (and will) because He is meeting our needs as only He knows them.

"Remember, your Father knows exactly what you need even before you ask him" (Matt. 6:8 TLB).

PRAY FOR ME

Dear Sir:

You don't know me, but I'm writing this letter to tell you that I read your book, *Prison to Praise*. I want to let you know that I am in Allegheny County Jail, Pittsburgh, Pennsylvania.

That's not what I want to tell you, that I am in jail. I want to say that when I read your book, the Lord was speaking to me. The reason I say this is because I am in the United States Army, and I committed a crime while being AWOL. That is why I am in here now. As I read your book, a strange feeling came over me. I closed my eyes and began to think, and while I was thinking, the thought came into my head, "Lord, what is it You want of me?" And as I kept thinking, it seemed as if the Lord had answered me through my thoughts by saying, "Put your faith in Me. Let Me guide you, and everything will be all right."

My real reason for writing to you is to ask you to help me. My faith is weak. I read my Bible every night, and I try during the day to keep my faith, but something is wrong. I don't know what. I know that I need Jesus, and I want Him. I realize that only He can help me. I would like to ask a favor of you, and that is to *pray for me* and ask Jesus to guide me. I want Him to come into my heart as my personal Savior. I pray, and sometimes I think that I have accepted the Lord, and other times I just don't know.

I believe that Jesus has done all the things that you said in your book that He did for you, and I want His help badly, and I need it. So please pray for me and ask Him to make me understand and to guide me. *I need help*

My Comments

It was in this very jail that the bars first slammed shut on me. God opened them for me, and He can for many more young men like this boy. Please lift those in the prisons of the United States in prayer and believe that God will continue to bring Christ to them.

"Let the sighing of the prisoner come before thee" (Ps. 79:11).

MINISTERING PRAISE TO OTHERS

Dear Colonel Carothers:

A young girl, about thirty and single, started coming to our church, seeking a solution to her problems, rather than seeking Him who is the answer. One evening she made a commitment, but found it hard to live up to, and her life was slowly going downhill. She needed a job and couldn't find one; her forthcoming marriage was falling apart with arguments all the time, until she was terribly nervous. Her fiancé was not a Christian, and had no inclinations along that line. She had had an automobile accident a few months before and still had to wear a back brace. Until the accident suit was settled, she could not collect any compensation from insurance, and so was getting way over her head in debt.

Things looked very black for her, and so one evening she called me, mainly, I believe, looking for an ear into which she could pour out her troubles. But our Lord had other ideas, and during the conversation, she asked me if I was going to our Tuesday-night meeting. Before she could say that she was not going, I asked her to pick me up. After I hung up the phone, doubts assailed me as to the loving-kindness I had shown (or not shown) in letting her use her car, knowing how short on funds she was, but I put it out of my mind, figuring that if God had wanted it to happen differently, He surely could have arranged it.

She came for me, nearly an hour early. She began to enumerate, for the umpteenth time, all her troubles, and I was praying in the Spirit for God to show me what to say in answer to her. It turned out that He didn't want me to "say" anything to her, but, by the Spirit, I was led to ask her to kneel with me in prayer. I began by *thanking God* that she was so far in debt, that her marriage was probably off, and that she couldn't find a job. I thanked Him for everything in her life. Then I stopped and looked at her.

She was kneeling there, eyes open, and mouth, too, in astonishment. I quoted her the Scripture that tells us to give thanks in *all* things. She did, reluctantly, not with a thankful heart, but she did it.

We went on to the prayer meeting, and that very night, the minister laid hands on her, and Jesus baptized her in the Holy Ghost and she spoke in tongues. Praise God! His ways are truly wonderful! As she has come to understand what God has really done for her and to accept His tender love for her, things have started to happen in her life. When she told her fiancé the things that had taken place in her spiritual life, he showed his true, unregenerate nature, and the engagement was broken, to the mutual benefit of both. She has a job in a doctor's office that she likes very much, and one of the couples in this part of His Body gave her $400 to clear up the unpaid debts. How can anyone doubt His love?

In my own life, every day is filled with small miracles, as I give God thanks for things, good or seemingly bad, for I *know* all things do, absolutely, work together for my good. I am a secretary at a home for alcoholics, and I have seen God redeem men through this very prayer put in action.

My Comments

As God has taught me to teach others about praising Him for everything, He is now teaching many people how to teach others. As a pebble dropped in the water results in ever-widening circles, so the ministry of praise reaches out through all the world. You can have your part in ministering to others.

"But thou art holy, O thou that inhabitest the praises of Israel" (Ps. 22:3).

FROM A PASTOR

Dear Rev. Carothers,

I really would like to learn to praise God like your books say, but I get terribly tired trying to be spiritual. I understand that being good is not what God has asked of us, but I know He does want us to care about other people's spiritual needs. At times, I get to the place where I don't care whether people become Christians or not. I try with all my might to tell them about Christ, but they so often don't want to hear. When I have worked and worked and see no solid results, I want to go off to a desert island and just be by myself.

But this reaction makes me feel even worse. I feel guilty that I'm so far from God that I can get to the place where I do not want to help people. This sort of split personality bothers me, and I would like to have any advice you can give me. Since I'm so easily discouraged, do you think I should leave my position as a minister and serve as a Christian layman?

My Comments

If you were "spiritual" more than you are, what do you think might happen? While traveling back and forth from one end of the country to another with meetings nearly every night of the week, crowds packing every facility I was invited to speak in, people always wanting me to do more than I felt capable of doing, and with very little sleep, I was all at once aware that I didn't want to help anyone. I, too, wanted to get away from it all and live a quiet life. When I realized how selfish my thoughts were, I felt guilty, but still didn't know what to do about it. I started thanking God that I felt exactly as I did. Almost immediately, understanding flowed into my mind. I realized that I, Merlin Carothers, am by nature not a "spiritual" person. This is exactly why I need Jesus to work in me! His Spirit has to accomplish everything good, and I can do nothing anyhow. Realizing this, I felt joy flowing within. I had something exciting to tell people, and I wanted to tell them! The tiredness was gone!

"I myself no longer live, but Christ lives in me. And the real life I now have within this body is a result of my trusting in the Son of God, who loved me and gave himself for me" (Gal. 2:20 TLB).

NEGATIVISM

Dear Chaplain Carothers,

I realize that you must get a great deal of mail from appreciative and inspired readers of your books, but I feel I must join them in sending a short note of thanks for the inspiration I have received through reading *Prison to*

Praise and *Power in Praise*. I have been a Christian just about all of my life, and for that time, twenty-two years, I have been exposed to and raised in a very negative Christianity—a life of forever trying to live like Jesus, but always feeling it was beyond the realm of human possibility.

After a score of years, including three years of Bible college, God is just now, in His magnificent love and mercy, teaching me a new way—the true way—*a positive life in Christ.* Having been called into His ministry some six years ago, I am at this time waiting for God's leading and guidance into that ministry—now with excitement at having a fully positive message to bring to a people besieged with negativism. It is through beautiful books like yours that God is teaching me so much. Thank you from my heart for letting God use you in such a beautiful way. May He continue to bless you richly.

My Comments

The Law said "Do this—Do that—Don't do this and don't do that." The Law was good, and its rules were from God. But God saw that man could never love Him if he had to live under laws that he couldn't keep no matter how hard he tried, so Christ fulfilled the requirements of the law and released us to love God. Now, because of our love for God, we can do His will out of the desires of our heart! He who tries to teach you what you ought to do must first teach you to love God. If he has not done that, he has no right to teach you what you ought to do!

I have met and been contacted by literally thousands of people who were raised in a religious church and home where many virtues were exalted as being Christianity in themselves. As young people, they were forced into a mold of "being good," and they accepted this as what "being a Christian" meant. But then comes the first step out into the world as it really is, and the young man or woman feels unable to live up to some of the do's and don'ts they have heard all their lives. They turn against religion of any kind and consider it for people too old to enjoy life.

I am not urging parents not to teach children what is right and wrong—far from it—nor am I advocating that you young people abandon what your Christian parents have taught you. I am saying that Christianity is not negativism as this young lady heard it was. The Good News of the Gospel is what God has done for us. Before we "do anything," He wants us to love Him. If your theology has not caused you to love God, I suggest you change your theology.

Have you read articles where some declare, "Beware of those who say, 'All you have to do is believe in Christ'?" This makes it sound as if believing in Jesus wasn't very important! Of course God is interested in our living right, but He was the one who made salvation dependent upon our faith in His Son. Be extremely careful never to belittle God's own plan of salvation. Belief in Christ is what changes men!

"This Good News tells us that God makes us ready for heaven—makes us right in God's sight—when we put our faith and trust in Christ to save us" (Rom. 1:17 TLB).

HUSBAND GONE

Dear Rev. Carothers,

I just am in the process of reading your book, *Prison to Praise*, and halfway through I felt I must write to you with a prayer request.

My husband is an alcoholic and has left our three daughters and me to live alone. I know he feels the guilt associated with drinking—and the sins of adultery that usually go along with it. He is a Christian—or at least I'm *almost* positive he had an experience with Christ several years ago—but now he has pulled far away and will talk to no one from our church.

My big hang-up was doubting that the Lord would "push Himself" on anyone who didn't make the first step. Then I read your book recounting experiences of prayer for unbelievers who had fantastic conversions even though their spirits were rebelling against Christ. And, of course, I was reminded of the apostle Paul—he certainly was not seeking Christ on the Road to Damascus.

So, I praise the Lord for leading me to your book. We love our husband and father and want him home, healed and whole—and loving his Lord. Our two older girls are both new Christians and pray for their daddy so fervently. I just pray the Lord will return my husband to me. I love him so and miss him. The Lord has been good to me, bringing me courage and comfort since my husband left. I pray, too, that I might receive the Holy Spirit soon.

My Comments

Yes! Remember Paul. He watched Stephen die just as he had watched many men die. But what was Stephen doing? He was praising the Lord! His praise reached Paul's unbelieving heart. Your praise can reach anyone, regardless of what they believe or are doing. God is faithful to His promise. His law of free will is not nearly as powerful as His law of praise. Praise does influence man's will!

"Giving thanks always for all things unto God and the Father in the name of our Lord Jesus Christ" (Eph. 5:20).

104

OVERWEIGHT/SEPARATED

Dear Rev. Carothers,*

My husband is no closer to coming home than he was, but my prayers for him are now for his salvation rather than for my own comfort. I am able to let God do the rest.

I am overcoming my eating habits that I wrote you about. God is such a marvelous God. He has time for the dumbest prayers. I really praise Him all the time now. I'm thankful He didn't make it easy for me like I wanted Him to. I can't thank you enough for opening a new door to God for me. I just praise Him for leading me to your books.

My Comments

"Make it easier for me" is often the cry of the person under Satan's attack. The cry should be "Make me aware that you are supplying me with what I need."

"My God shall supply all your need" (Phil. 4:19).

*This letter was from a lady who was so depressed over her husband's leaving her and her inability to control a bad overweight problem that she was prepared to commit suicide. I sent her a copy of *Power in Praise* and invited her to be thankful for her problems.

BAPTISM

Dear Chaplain Carothers,

I've begun this letter for two real important reasons. I wanted first of all to thank you for writing *Prison to Praise* and to thank God for giving me the opportunity to read it! I want also to see if this message of mine will really reach you. I must know you are a real person and that you have received my letter. For some reason, I don't think my obsession will end until I know you exist as a fact.

I had heard of speaking in tongues from the friend who gave me your book. I've had doubts about *it*, too. I am Catholic, and am ashamed to say I've never heard of this type of praying before. I know of some Catholics who practice this type of praying, but I'm not familiar with any of the Church teachings concerning it. I'll have to find that out for myself. I've always held fast to the thought that there was something more to worshiping than attending once-a-week service. Your book has actually given me new confidence in my beliefs.

My Comments

All over the nation people are feeling this powerful force urging them to learn more about the power of God than they have been hearing in their particular church. People of all denominations are saying, "I want to know that God is for real." His power is moving in many people's lives, and He will reveal Himself to you, too! When He moves in you, through the Holy Spirit, others will say of you, "Is he/she for real? No one can be that happy."

"Be filled with the Spirit ... singing and making melody in your heart" (Eph. 5:18,19).

FARMER'S WIFE IN FIELD

An Indiana farmer's wife accepted the dual role that farmers' wives often have. At planting and harvest times, she spent a big part of every day on a tractor. As she rode hour after hour over mile-long rows, her continual burden was the thought of how much she needed to be doing in the house. She was the mother of three children, active in church, school, and community work, and never had enough time—even when she wasn't helping her husband.

The long rows never seemed to end! She heard me talking about praising the Lord for all things. When she went back to the field, she started praising the Lord, singing, laughing, and blessing the crops. The hours became shorter and shorter. And the days were gone before she even remembered what she could be doing in the house. At the end of her first day with this new attitude, her husband said, "I can't believe that you got as much done in the field today as you did."

She responded, "I didn't really; God came along and flew me over the rows before I even knew it." For the rest of the season, she kept marveling at the joy God gave her when she thanked Him for each day as it was.

"No man, having put his hand to the plow, and looking back, is fit for the kingdom of God" (Luke 9:62).

SICKNESS

Dear Sir,

I am from a Methodist background and had heard very little about God healing people in this day. When I heard you talk about praising God even for sickness, I did not think that I would ever be able to do such a thing.

I'm getting on in years and normally am not surprised when aches and pains come into these bones of mine. But several months ago I began having a back pain that just wouldn't quit. It grew more and more painful. I was never able to be free from its domination over everything I tried to do. I was frequently awakened at night with the pain, and the discomfort increased to the point that it was very difficult for me to get out of bed in the morning. I confess that at times my fears grew as I thought of the possibility of being completely incapacitated by this pain. I went to several doctors.

One morning when I awoke, I felt even more pain than I had previously. The thought flashed through my mind that I had never once been thankful to God for this experience nor had I ever tried to believe that He would teach me something wonderful out of this. I began praising God and thanking Him for the physical pain I was enduring. This didn't help a bit; it was still very difficult for me to get out of bed. I moved around for a little while, and then felt that I had to sit down.

While sitting in an easy chair, I meditated on thanking and praising God. It seemed like I was filled with a deep sense of praise to God. I felt praise for God that I had never experienced before. I felt a kind of joy coming up inside of me. I ended up by actually being thankful for the pain I had been enduring. When I realized that it was time for me to get up and get something done, I thought, "I'm going to believe that God will just bless and help me all day long and teach me whatever it is He wants me to learn."

When I got out of my chair and started to move around, I was suddenly aware that I had no pain. I moved my arms and legs and then bent over. To my astonishment, the pain was gone. I had never seen a miracle of any kind in my life. I thank God for letting me see His wonderful power. I may have pains in the future, but now I know for sure that God uses everything and will bless us as we trust Him.

My Comments

Not everyone is so completely and dramatically relieved of pain as this woman has been, but God has His perfect plan for each one of us. (This woman is now quietly sharing with people in her group the joy of what has happened in her life. Those who had known her for many years had never seen a healing before. They are now interested in learning for themselves what God can do for them. Each of us plays a small part in God's glorious plan to reveal His love for all men.)

"He that spared not his own Son, but delivered him up for us all, how shall he not with him also freely give us all things?" (Rom. 8:32).

SON SENTENCED TO LIFE IN PRISON

At times people believe and praise the Lord only until they either receive what they want or become convinced they will not get it. This attitude corrupts the soul and holds back many of God's blessings. One family that I know was determined to trust God whatever happened. Their son was arrested and charged with a very serious crime. They called me frequently and asked for prayer. The mother was forced to leave home and live in another state in order to be near their imprisoned son as he waited for his trial. Delays stretched on and on for months, but the family kept believing God and expecting Him to work good out of the whole situation. As the conclusion seemed to be getting farther away, and the trial looked no closer than at the very beginning, I advised the mother to go home and leave her son in God's hands.

When the trial finally came, the verdict was "Guilty" and the young son was sentenced to life in prison. I immediately wondered what this would do to the persistent faith of the parents. My confidence in God's people was greatly encouraged when I next saw the parents. Their faith did not falter! They were still confident that God was working out His perfect will for their son! They reaffirmed that their central desire was that God should draw their beloved boy to Himself. He had their earnest prayer that He would do it in exactly the right way.

How different this was from many anguished parents to whom I have had the opportunity to minister. So often their faith reaches only as far as they can see. If God doesn't move where they can see, they crumble in despair and give vent to the most self-pitying emotions they can find. Their sorrow eats their insides out, and there is no peace, rest, or hope. To them, God seems to be weak and powerless. And their lack of faith collects ever-increasing sadness as the years pass by.

———————

"Do ye look on these things after the outward appearance?" (II Cor. 10:7).

I AM GUILTY

Dear Sir,

Before my husband went to Vietnam, he was spending most of his nights with another woman. He laughed about it when I begged him to stop, and he said she was much better to be with than I was. She was not married, had a good job, and did not want to get married. He said she enjoyed spending the night with him, and he was going to enjoy it as often as he could. The unbelievable part about the whole thing was that on Sunday we would go to his parents' church and act as if nothing was wrong.

I should have done something before he went to Vietnam, but I didn't know what to do. I kept believing that he would change, and that our marriage would be saved. He said he didn't love me, but would keep the marriage going for his parents' sake. They are very religious and would be quite upset over a divorce in the family.

While my husband was in Vietnam, I met a man who gave me the kindness and understanding I have not received during my three years of marriage. At first we only talked, and I told him what had been happening in my marriage. But then we got too involved, and I became pregnant. He advised me to get a divorce, regardless of what my husband's parents might think.

When my husband came home, I was showing, and all hell broke loose. He dragged me in front of his parents and revealed what a "wicked wife" I was. They quickly spread the word to everyone in the church and the community. When I told the family what my husband had done before he went to Vietnam, they said I was making it all up to save my own skin. My own family is humiliated. I feel like I have betrayed everyone. The only solution I can see is to take a car and drive it off a cliff.

Everyone I know would be relieved to have me out of the way. Even the man who made me pregnant is afraid of what might happen to him if I tell anyone who he is. Would I go to hell if I kill myself? I do believe in Christ, but that doesn't help me know what to do.

Dear Friend,

If you kill yourself, you will be falling right into the devil's trap. He has used your husband, his family, and the man involved to destroy you. If you kill yourself, the devil will be the only one to profit. Jesus died to save you. He lives to save you. He wants to fill your life with joy and peace, and He will still do this if you will trust Him.

Your greatest need at this moment is to be filled with His Holy Spirit. He will then lead you into the right decision. No human is wise enough to tell you exactly what you should do now. Many people will be quick to give you free advice, but they would probably be wrong. Let God through His Spirit guide you. This entire experience can bring you to a wonderful relationship with God that you might never have had! When this is clear to you, you will be glad for everything.

Most of all, know that God loves you just as you are! Please find people in your community who know what it means to be baptized in the Holy Spirit.

If you would like to telephone me, please do. If you so desire, I will find someone near you who knows about being led by the Holy Spirit.

My Comments

She was an adulteress. She was guilty, caught in the act. There was no doubt about it. They saw her; they knew; they were right. They brought her to Jesus along with all their facts. God had said she should be stoned to death. This wasn't a church law or a doctrine of man, this was God's law! By God's own plan, she had to be pronounced guilty and killed.

Their facts were right. They knew the law. The woman was guilty. There was nothing to discuss or debate—but one thing! Who was to stone her? Jesus did not disagree with their facts, He only revealed what they did not know about God's law!

Before they came into Jesus' presence, they were bold, brave, eager to condemn In His presence, something happened to them. She was guilty, but they left in shame. They had convicted her when they had no right to judge. Why not? They had God's own Word behind them! She was the guilty one, but they were found guilty.

She introduced a new law into the world that is still understood by very few. Only those who have no guilt are free to condemn others. Have you been condemned by others? Have their cries for your conviction caused you to fall to Jesus' feet for forgiveness? If so, then you can be glad for their condemnation. It has brought you to Christ. But now they are gone, and you are alone with Him. Now He says, "Neither do I condemn you. Go and sin no more."

If you had not come into Jesus' presence, you would still be hearing and feeling the bite of their sarcastic condemnation. And when they are right, it hurts even more. But now you come to Jesus. They may be trailing behind or dragging you helplessly along, but you have come, and now you are free! Your guilt is the same, but the condemnation is gone. He has forgiven you!

"As far as God is concerned there is a sweet, wholesome fragrance in our lives. It is the fragrance of Christ within us" (II Cor. 2:15 TLB).

THE LAST LAUGH

Dear Rev. Carothers:

I feel as if I am drowning. I have been sick for a long while and am getting sicker. I can't even take care of my own home. My three children go from one sickness to another. My husband has been out of work for a long while, and we are trying to make it on welfare. We never laugh anymore, and it seems that every day is a little worse than the day before. God forgive me, but I've been thinking the only way out was for me to shoot the children and then myself. I thought my husband might make it on his own if he could leave this area and find a job.

I've been given a shot of new hope by reading your books, *Prison to Praise* and *Power in Praise*. A neighbor loaned them to me. Would you pray for us? I believe you know God in a special way, and He would listen to you.

Dear Friend,

Think of yourself in a deep canyon with steep walls going up both sides. Then think of a dam being built at the lower end and the water beginning to rise in the valley. What would happen to you if you stayed there? The paths you were able to freely walk on before would soon be covered with water. It would rise until it was over your head. You would swim as long as you could, and then you would drown.

Satan has you in that valley and is using the problems of life to drown you. He has discovered how to get at you and will continue until you learn how to reverse the tables on him. I will be in prayer that as you read this letter you will be able to leave that valley. Through the power of the Holy Spirit, I believe you are free! You and your family can now come into a new life in Christ! Our

114

faith in Him will never fail. Let me know when you are free. Remember that you would never have asked for prayer if these troubles had not come to you.

Dear Rev. Carothers:

As I read your letter, something happened in me. I believed! I saw what Satan had done to me. I had once been a Christian but had given up. With many tears I asked Jesus to forgive me. He did, and a wonderful feeling came all over me. I felt well again, even in body! When my children came home, I prayed with them. They thought I was drunk at first, but laughed and laughed, in a very good way, when they saw I really wanted to pray.

By the time my husband got home, we were all laughing and singing. He hadn't seen me laugh for a long while. He agreed to pray with me, and he started to laugh too.

You may think I am giving you a fairy tale, but soon after this, my husband got his first job in over a year. We are getting back on our feet and giving Christ all the credit. Thank you for your book telling us to praise Him.

My Comments

Picture another dam at the end of a valley. Start filling it with living water. Jesus said, "Out of your belly shall flow rivers of living water." As the water of praise rises, Satan is caught in a trap. He must either leave or drown. He cannot stand praise. God dwells in our praises, and Satan cannot stand to be around you when you praise God. You now have the solution as to how to get rid of him.

"Fear not: for I have redeemed thee, I have called thee by name; thou art mine. . . . The rivers, they shall not overflow thee. . . . For I am the Lord thy God" (Isa. 43:1-3).

HARD OF HEARING

Dear Sir,

I feel as though I could write a book on the marvels of God's goodness and love from my own personal experiences. But, keep on smiling, I won't bore you with a book!

I just finished reading your *Prison to Praise*. In the last chapter, you point out that we can find a reason for praise in anything that happens to us. I'm not sure that I would say, "Praise the Lord," if I fell off a ladder and broke my leg, but if I may be personal, I can point out that handicaps can prove to be a blessing.

For twenty years I have been handicapped with a hearing loss, which in the last two years became so severe that I had to wear two hearing aids turned up to full volume in order to hear what was being talked about in my Sunday-school class, or in company. I can now say, "Praise God," for this, because since I could derive no pleasure from watching and listening to TV, I had to turn to my silent friends, books, and I read dozens of them. They gave me a much clearer insight into some of the Scriptures which I had read often, but never really studied. What a revelation!

Today, as a result of praise, I can say, "Praise the Lord." I hear quite distinctly with only one hearing aid turned down to its lowest level. There is more—much more—which the Lord has done for me personally in the physical realm. But this is nothing compared to what happened to me in the spiritual realm. When I hear the beautiful chorus, "He touched me, oh, He touched me—and oh, the joy that floods my soul! Something happened, and now I know, He touched me and made me whole," I want to confess with tears, "Praise God, it happened to me."

Forgive me if I seem to be holding myself up as the epitome of physical and spiritual perfection. I'm still only a sinner, saved by grace. "This is my story, to God be the glory: I'm only a sinner saved by grace," but also a sinner who shed the mask of phoniness, because in love, He touched me.

As I write this, it is a dark, dreary, miserably cold day outside, for which I can also say, "Thank the Lord," because it gives me a day in which I can read, listen to inspiring music and tapes, and concentrate on God's love as put forth in His Word.

My Comments

A rich spirit is often the result of physical infirmities. The writer of this letter has very obviously permitted her infirmity, through praise, to work for her greater joy.

"The Lord is great, and greatly to be praised" (Ps. 96:4).

BACK ON PRAISE

Dear Rev. Carothers,

Right in front of me, I saw my own testimony. In *Power in Praise*, you wrote the account of how I had learned to praise God. As I read what I had already told you, my heart was overcome with remorse. I remembered how I had so completely given my life to God and had been filled with such joyful faith. But then I had started to feel sorry for myself again, and the joy gradually left.

Thank you for reminding me of what God did for me! As I gave my life back to God, the old joy came flooding into me. I'm even able to be thankful that I lost it, for I appreciate it even more now! Whatever God does with my life now is up to Him. I'm going to be thankful whatever happens. I accept the peace Jesus offered.

117

My Comments

When this dear lady saw her own testimony in print in *Power in Praise*, she was reminded of the wonderful things God had already done for her. This is a very strong reminder to each one of us that no matter how far we progress up the ladder of praise, there is always the possibility of our sliding back down into the clouds of darkness. After you have learned to be thankful and praise God, be mindful that Satan will always be watching for an opportunity to interject doubt or fear. He will wait to try to catch you at your weakest moment.

Perhaps it would be a very good idea for you to sit down and write your own testimony of praise and thanksgiving for what God has done for you. Place it in your Bible, and have it available at any time in the future when you are tempted to believe that something in your life is worthy of giving you discouragement. Your own testimony, as well as that of other people, is able to confirm your faith in what God has done for you.

"Peace I leave with you, my peace I give unto you: not as the world giveth, give I unto you. Let not your heart be troubled, neither let it be afraid" (John 14:27).

OUT OF FELLOWSHIP

Dear Sir,

I have needed to share my problem with someone, but had no one I felt I could trust. I have read your books, *Prison to Praise* and *Power in Praise*, and have felt strongly led to write and ask for your advice. I feel as if you would understand.

118

I was at one time one of the leading members in my church. I taught one of the largest Sunday-school classes, was in charge of our youth program, sang in our choir, and often sang special solos. I was often referred to by the pastor and other people as one of the happiest Christians they had ever known. People often said things to me like, "You are the most loving Christian I have ever known."

No one in the church knew anything about my private life. At home my problems grew continually worse. We had three children before I discovered my husband was a homosexual. When I first found out, I was too shocked to even think. I could not believe it for a long time, even after he admitted it to me. I knew something was terribly wrong, because for over two years he had not wanted anything to do with me in a physical way. For a long while, I thought it might be my fault, so I did everything I could think of to make myself attractive. Frequently I begged him to come to bed with me, but for over two years he evaded every advance I made.

My husband finally confessed that he could no longer be a husband to me because I no longer interested him. He said his desire for other men was so strong that he could not be interested in any woman. When he said this, many things forced their way into my mind. I remembered several strange things I had seen him do, and my mind finally had to accept the terrible reality. After much persuasion, my husband went to a psychiatrist with me. The psychiatrist advised me there was little he could do, as my husband did not want to change.

My prayer life now revolved around my problem. Over and over I asked God to help me know what to do. When my husband came home late at night, I would know where he had been, and the thought of what he had been doing literally made me vomit. The house seemed to be filled with evil the moment he came through the door. Panic gripped me when he even came near me. When he put his arms around our sons, I screamed inside, "Oh God, don't let him make homosexuals out of our sons."

When I received the baptism in the Holy Spirit, I learned that my husband's problem was probably spiritual and could be caused by Satan. My doctor said it could be caused by a hormone imbalance, but I wanted to do anything that might help. I prayed continually for God to cast out the evil thing and urged my husband to go with me to a minister for help. He insisted that in today's "enlightened society," homosexuals were being accepted as "normal people."

Finally my heart was so broken, I filed for a divorce, and he agreed to it. It was the only thing I knew to do to retain my own sanity. I felt clean before God, but I realize that I could have been wrong. I guess what I want you to do first is to tell me what you think I should have done. But even more, I need your advice as to what I should do about my church.

When the people of our church heard that I had filed for a divorce they descended upon me in force, and I was bombarded with questions. They insisted that there were no "Bible grounds" for divorce but adultery. Had my husband committed adultery? they wanted to know. Every time the phone rang, I knew it would be one of the church people or the pastor urging me to not get a divorce. They insisted that whatever the problem was, God would help us work it out. They came to my home and nearly drove me out of my mind with their continual questioning. What had my husband done? Why did I believe it was right for me to get a divorce?

Is this the way you are? Do you keep probing into other people's business? Has my church been fair with me? They wanted me to resign my Sunday-school class. So I did. I would go to another church, but this is the only church in our community where my children will learn about the Bible.

What should I do? Tell them all what my husband is? If I do, my own children will be too humiliated to stay in the same town. Wherever they go, the news could follow them. Would the church care anything about my children?

Dear Friend in Christ,

I apologize to you for all that has been done to you in the name of Christ. Well-meaning people are often driven by an inner compulsion to know everything about everyone else. Even though their intentions may have been good, they have greatly wronged you. When you needed their love, they displayed their own self-righteousness. They ignored Jesus' stern warning never to judge other people.

I cannot tell you whether you were right or wrong to get a divorce. I do not have the right to tell you what is God's will for you. His Spirit is here to lead you, and He is faithful if we do the best we can to be led by Him. Now that you have made your decision, do not let it give you guilt or fear. Tell God that if you were wrong, you ask for His forgiveness. Then go on to build a life for your children and yourself.

I recommend that you leave your church—at least for now. Perhaps time will heal the wounds you feel. Another church may receive you with love, and this is what you need at this time. Remember that Jesus loves you and is always with you. Trust Him, and He will never let you down.

Your great opportunity now is to thank God for everything that has happened to you. Be thankful that you married the man you did. Rejoice that the church acted so self-righteously. Believe that God is using each of these things to bless you and your children. Do not ask how. Believe that He *is*. He has opened your life to new understanding. You, like everyone else, need Jesus more than ever! Problems have forced you to seek His love. You have seen how weak and fallible people are. You, too, are "people." Your own mistakes are not as obvious to you, but you, like others, need God's forgiving grace. All sins are horribly black to Him, and each of us can only trust in Christ's cleansing blood!

Dear Rev. Carothers,

What a joy your letter is to me! I immediately began to thank God for myself as I am. My continual weeping has turned into peace. I now believe that God does love me. My anger has left me, and I'm even able to be thankful when little things go wrong. I have a lot to learn, but I believe I'm started. I'm reading *Prison to Praise* again, and I'm only now understanding what you meant. Please keep praying for me. I haven't found a church yet, but I believe I will.

My Comments

Religious people flung the woman taken in adultery at Jesus' feet. She was guilty, but worst of all, they were pleased to be able to declare her guilty. Only those who feel they are clean before God are able to bring railing accusations against others. A sinner bows his head and says, "God be merciful to me a sinner." Many of you have probably been in situations in which others felt perfectly justified in judging you. Do not let their weakness discourage you. Be thankful for them, and trust God to use them to strengthen your love for Jesus. Think of how He, in all His purity, could hang on the cross and say about those who crucified Him, "Father, forgive them, for they do not know what they are doing." If He could forgive those men, surely you and I can forgive the mistakes that others make about us. More than that! We can love them and ask God to forgive them!

"Forgive us our debts, as we forgive our debtors" (Matt. 6:12).

SMOKING

Dear Sir,

I have the terribly bad habit of smoking. Every time I try to quit, I gain weight. I'm overweight now and can't afford to gain more. What do I do? I've tried thanking God for my smoking with the hope I would stop wanting to smoke, but it doesn't work. Could you pray for me like you did the soldier, so I won't be able to smoke anymore?

Dear Friends,

What is a bad habit? It is anything that is bad for you. Which is the most harmful to you, overeating or smoking? You are probably not a very good authority on this. Ask your doctor what he thinks in your case. I estimate that in nine cases out of ten he would say that overweight will kill you faster than smoking. So, I recommend that you accept a completely different outlook on your bad habits. If you lose one, you pick up another—like eating instead of smoking. Why not give the habits to God and let Him, through Christ, take them away from you? Then Christ will receive all the credit. If He receives the credit for taking them away, you should not accept the blame for having them. Your feeling of guilt is the very thing that holds back your faith to believe Him. You feel unworthy because of your own weakness, therefore unworthy for Him to heal your weaknesses.

Give both habits—plus any others you may be aware of—to Christ. Believe that He accepts them, and you no longer have them. When any thought to the contrary comes to you, recognize that it is coming from Satan, who wants to discredit every promise that Christ made to you. "Come unto me all ye that labor and are heavy laden, and I will give you rest" (Matt. 11:28). Satan wants you to deny that the habits are gone, so you will be unable to give Christ the glory for keeping His promise to you. As Jesus said to the two blind men, "As your faith, so be it unto you."

When you finish reading this, agree with me that both habits are gone, and I believe they will be.

A recent phone call indicated they were! Hundreds of people are being totally delivered from bad habits by faith in Jesus. The worse the habit, the less capable you are of ending it. But your weakness becomes His strength—when you give it to Him! If you believe this, you can even be thankful for your bad habits.

"Then it will be as though I had sprinkled clean water on you, for you will be clean—your filthiness will be washed away . . . and I will give you a new heart—I will give you new and right desires" (Ezek. 36:25,26 TLB).

I'M IN JAIL

Dear Sir:

You don't know me, but I sure know you. I've gotten in some trouble. Well, here's my story. I needed money because I wanted to get a motorcycle. My brother has one, and I wanted to be like him. So two other boys and I went on a robbing spree. We robbed four bars and taverns. Then I got caught with the stuff at my house. After a hearing, I was brought down to the Allegheny County Jail in Pittsburgh, Pa. I've been here for close to two months now.

I went to see the chaplain, Mr. Simon, and I asked him for a Bible. So he gave me a New Testament. He also showed me another book, that was about you. (*Prison to Praise* was the name of it). I read all the chapters except the last. My eyes were tired of reading, so I put the book down and walked outside my cell and sat down. While I was sitting down, something told me to read that last chapter. It kept in my mind for five or ten minutes. Then I went and read it. It was the best chapter of the whole book. I really believe in God since I read that book.

Now I'm reading the Bible from beginning to end. The first verse I ever learned out of the Bible was John 3:16. I thanked God for what happened to me, and I know He'll help me every way He can. What I would like for you to do is to pray for me often as you can. I'm praying for probation. This is my first time in criminal court, and I pray for the best.

My Comments

I do not know if this boy's parents have been able to believe that God was using a prison cell to help their son. God took a book, about praise, and used it to win a very lost boy to His Son. Your praise can reach into the darkest corners of the world and lead people to a new life in Christ! You may never see or hear of the results, but God does! The next time you are placed under stress by some difficult circumstance, remember that God could use your praise to help someone. Your act of praise at that moment is a release of faith, and it is the power of faith that God uses. Can you see why He has urged us to praise Him continually?

"Let the people praise thee, O God; let all the people praise thee. Then ... God, even our own God, shall bless us" (Ps. 67:5,6).

OVERWEIGHT

Brother Carothers in Jesus Christ,

I just finished reading your book, *Prison to Praise*. I could not put it down—I read and read.

Like a thunderbolt, the application of thanksgiving and

125

praise shook me and got my attention! I have a serious overweight problem. I weigh 330 pounds or thereabouts. I've battled it ever since I was seven years old (I'm twenty-six now). I've known I'm eating my grave nearer and nearer. But I was helpless, trying to curb my eating. Now, just a few short minutes ago, I lifted my voice in praise, thanking God for this 150 pounds of ugly fat. Joy just flowed over, and I started laughing, not caring that it was 12:30 in the morning, that my husband was sleeping in the next room! I just praised God and thanked Him.

I *expect* a miracle to unfold. It has already began to unfold. A miracle of healing in my body and the loss of the ugly fat. And I praise God and thank Him for showing Himself to me in this. Praise God for your testimony and witness.

My Comments

Later communication with this woman has indicated marvelous changes in her body and personality. As she learned to thank God for her problem, the Holy Spirit enabled her to understand what had caused it, and what she could do about it. As she lost her ugly fat, she also lost many ugly ideas about herself, other people, and God. Even overweight can be turned into a blessing as we believe that God has permitted this problem to help us recognize an even greater need that we have. Too many people would like to be free of overweight without any cost to themselves or without learning any worthwhile lesson. Overweight is a major cause of unhappiness, poor health, and related diseases in the United States. What a glorious relief to know that God will bring healing, deliverance, and joy as His people begin to relinquish their praise to Him. Of course, God does not want His people to be unhealthy. But He does permit unhealthy appetites to attack us, in order that we may realize our deep poverty of soul.

"Bless the Lord, O my soul, and forget not all his benefits: Who forgiveth all thine iniquities; who healeth all thy diseases" (Ps. 103:2,3).

A RESPIRATORY DISEASE

Dear Rev. Carothers,

What blessings have flowed from your *Prison to Praise*? A friend sent me her copy last May, when a year-round, lifelong respiratory condition reached an extreme stage. My problem was so great that in spite of many other earthly blessings, I wanted to die. I don't mean that I just occasionally thought about it; it had become a force within me so strong that it dominated every other part of my life. I do not believe that I was over-emotional about my problem, I was simply tired out from fighting just to be able to breathe. Doctors could not help me; every known medication had been tried; changes in climate had not greatly improved my condition; nothing seemed to bring any relief. It was only in total desperation that I agreed to begin thanking and praising God for myself as I was. I really thought that there was nothing else that I could try anyhow. I might as well thank God. I am therefore aware that it was nothing good in me that caused me to begin praising God.

When I began to really praise God in my heart, for me as I am, I immediately noticed a change in my breathing. At first I thought I must be imagining it, for I knew—or at least thought I knew—that any kind of healing would take longer than that to take effect. But the more I praised God, the more I kept experiencing a change taking place in me. A lifetime of fighting to breathe began to be replaced by inward joy. It may seem hard to believe, but I was more excited about the spiritual change that was taking place than I was about the physical change. God was actually doing something for *me*! I had always thought of myself as being too insignificant for God to notice. I had heard many prayers for many people that never seemed to do any real good, and I had decided that God intervened only for very special people. But here I was, experiencing God Himself doing something for *me*. I cannot express what I felt.

Thank you for sharing *Power in Praise* with me. If I wrote on and on, I could not possibly express what it feels like to be sitting here writing to you, breathing normally and naturally, and filled with an inward peace that God loves me. Please share with everyone you can, the wonderful truth that God loves us all.

My Comments

There is no such thing as a little person in God's eyes. We are all important enough for Him to give His only Son for us. And with His Son, He freely gives us "all things."

"He hath put a new song in my mouth, even praise unto our God: many shall see it, and fear, and shall trust in the Lord" (Ps. 40:3).

TALK-TALK-TALK

Dear Rev Carothers,

I was scheduled to take an 800-mile trip with a lady who always annoyed me to tears with her continual stream of talking If one word was said about any subject, she launched into a discussion that covered every facet of that subject plus anything that might be remotely connected. My nerves sometimes stretched to the breaking point, even though I did my best to patiently cover up the agony I went through every time this woman was around.

Thinking about the 800-mile trip and the at least sixteen hours I was scheduled to be with this woman, was becoming more than I could bear. I tried to come up with an excuse that would help me to politely cancel the trip.

At the hairdressers, I casually picked up a book lying by the dryer and read about an Army chaplain who had been in all kinds of trouble. At first I nearly put it down, thinking, "This doesn't have anything to do with me," but something kept drawing me to read on. By the time my hair was dry, and I could have left, I was so absorbed in *Prison to Praise*, I couldn't leave. By the end, I knew what I was supposed to learn! I gave the forthcoming 800-mile trip to God and started praising Him for it. My anticipation increased, for I knew He was going to teach me something. I thought it was going to be about patience.

I was all wrong! The woman hardly opened her mouth the entire trip. She was friendly and cheerful, but had very little to say. It turned out to be the most interesting trip of my life. As a result, I'm practicing praising God in everything and seeing continued results! Thank you for sharing this marvelous secret with me.

My Comments

If God could close the mouths of lions, couldn't He easily close the mouth of one human? Or couldn't He close our ears? Or couldn't He fill us with such peace that we would enjoy whatever anyone had to say? The fact that He hasn't done this for you does not mean that He doesn't want to. Step boldly into every situation and believe He will be there to supply the *exact need*. Remember—not what you think He *ought to do*—but what you "need."

"He that spared not his own Son, but delivered him up for us all, how shall he not with him also freely give us all things?" (Rom. 8:32).

PLEASE DON'T PRAY FOR ME

Dear Rev. Carothers,

Through a serious accident, I received a permanent injury that is obvious to anyone who looks at me. At the very beginning, I believed God would heal me, and I welcomed anyone who wanted to pray for me. As the condition continued, my faith weakened, but people continued to come. When I hinted I would prefer they stay at home to pray for me, they often said I should believe and let them pray for me.

After several months, I started to dread the mere presence of anyone who believed in healing. Sooner or later they would want to lay hands on me and to pray. I even dreaded anyone coming to see me, because over and over they went through the same routine of asking me to believe God for my healing. My faith in Christ as my Savior began to get weaker. If God wouldn't heal me, how could I know for sure that He forgave me of my sins?

When I read your book, *Power in Praise*, I knew that I did not have to live under people's condemnation any more. Trusting in Christ as my Savior was again the important thing to me. Thank you for helping me to see this.

My Comments

Well-meaning Christians often drive the sick away from Jesus. I have seen this happen so often that I want to tell you something that is very important. Never pray for the sick in their presence unless they ask you or you are absolutely sure they want you to. Never! And don't put them in the awkward position of having to ward off your polite suggestion that they ought to ask you. Don't suggest it directly or indirectly unless you are in a position where you are sure they want you to pray. If one prayer, in Jesus' name, has been made, you have no authority to demand that people give you an opportunity to exercise your faith at their expense. Jesus Himself only prayed for those who came and asked for prayer or placed themselves in a position where He knew they wanted Him to pray. The disciples waited for people to ask! There is much we do not understand about healing, but we can understand the distress people feel when everyone wants to "lay hands on them." Better for a person to remain sick and keep their faith in Christ than to be pestered into losing all their faith.

"Lay hands suddenly on no man" (I Tim. 5:22).

MY HUSBAND OR . . .

Dear Chaplain,

I have wanted to be an instrument of God, but for some reason I can't completely submit to Him.

Right now I'm in a state of not knowing which way to turn—to my husband who has returned home after walking out when I was seven months pregnant, or to a man who has treated me and my children as if we were pure gold. My husband slapped me around whenever my opinion disagreed with his. He went off with another woman who stayed with him until she got tired of his hitting her.

The man who came to help my children and me is a fine Christian. He would be willing to share a religious home and take us to church. He wants to keep God alive

131

in the home.

I have no desire to stay with my husband, but some people have told me I should stay with him regardless of what he does to me. I don't know what God wants me to do. Please, I need your prayers to help me out of this mess and to know what God wants for me.

Dear Friend,

My prayers you have, but I have no advice as to what you should do. Many people always know what others should do. Their advice is cheap, and the quality of it is also. They want you to conform to their image of God—whatever that may be. I believe God is more interested in your love for Him than in what you do. If you listen to me or to others, you are not likely to hear what He has to say.

Make your decision in faith that God will work out what is best. He can change your husband into the man you would like him to be, or He can give you a good life with the man who offers to love you and your children.

When your husband gave himself to another woman, he gave you scriptural grounds for a divorce. But God has also taught us to forgive and trust Him to work out the desires of our heart. There is no written law to tell you what you must do, but you are surrounded by a God of love who wants to bless your life and help you in everything.

"When he, the Spirit of truth, is come, he will guide you into all truth" (John 16:13).

METHODIST MINISTER TRANSFERRED

Dear Reverend,

Yesterday, I was notified by our Pastor Parish Committee that they had requested I be transferred because of my interest in Pentecost. The old me would have been greatly disturbed, but I had just read your book, *Power in Praise*. Instead of being upset, I laughed and rejoiced that God was working in my life for some new and glorious purpose. I am filled with peace and thanksgiving that God loves me so much.

Thank you for sharing with me this wonderful good news that God works in all things. Also, thank you for sending the book to me. God bless you as you share these wonderful secrets with all His people.

My Comments

Bad news often affects us like being hit below the belt. When praise becomes a way of life, bad news is turned into joy. Why live in fear that bad news may come to you today when you can know that God is in charge of all your news?

"Giving thanks always for all things unto God and the Father in the name of our Lord Jesus Christ" (Eph. 5:20).

AN ALCOHOLIC CHANGED

Dear Rev. Carothers,

My husband and I were separated as a result of his many years of drinking. He was an alcoholic from the word "go." I knew he was sick, but I couldn't live with the violent rages he went into when he was drunk—and this was every day. For several years I lived as an alcoholic widow. Self-pity over my lot in life was a continual part of everything I did or thought about.

Then a friend told me she thought I needed to read a book called *Prison to Praise*. I agreed to read it. By the last page, I agreed to thank God for my life as it was. A rest came over me I had never experienced before. People may find this hard to believe, but the very next day my husband called me. He said, "I accepted Christ last night, and believe I am going to be okay now." We started meeting to talk, and I could see that he was different. We are back together now, and I cannot tell you how glad I am that God helped you to write that book.

My Comments

While in California, I had the opportunity to pray with this man to receive the baptism in the Holy Spirit. It was difficult to perceive that he had once been an alcoholic.

"He died for our sins just as God our Father planned, and rescued us from the evil world in which we live" (Gal. 1:4 TLB).

NOTHING BUT UNHAPPINESS

Dear Rev. Carothers,

I heard you talk about praising God in everything, and then I read your book. I've tried to practice your idea, but it doesn't work for me. No matter what I do, we are always too poor to have anything. I work all the time to try and get ahead, but the harder I work, the worse everything gets. Does God want me to work all my life and never have any joy? You seem to have nothing but joy, and I have nothing but unhappiness. Is this fair?

Dear Friend,

If praise were my idea, I am sure it would never work. Since praise is God's idea, it always works. It changes either the situation or us or both. But even if it did nothing, this one verse should always be remembered: "The Lord, who is worthy to be praised: so shall I be saved from mine enemies" (II Sam. 22:4).

I believe God will prosper you, and He will fill you with His joy as you trust and believe Him, but please keep in mind the important conclusion Job reached after great affliction had been poured upon him by Satan. He said, "He performeth the thing that is appointed for me" (Job 23:14). What a change this makes in our lives when we believe it! How differently we look upon the many things that tend to irritate us. Our duties become a joy. How is it possible? Because God is in everything, He permits it all to be so. It does not matter, then, what comes. Think of the glory in this. God is working out the things "appointed for" you.

"But he knoweth the way that I take: when he hath tried me, I shall come forth as gold" (Job 23:10).

MISSIONARY SON

Dear Brother Carothers,

I have read with great interest your two books. The Lord has challenged me to practice praise in the most difficult problems in my life.

I am a missionary here in the Bahamas and meet so many who need this message. Is it possible for us to praise *for* another person and expect these miracles—when the person is not interested and far away?

I have begun to do this for my son who is so deceived by college teaching and influence.

Dear Parent,

The most powerful form of prayer is the prayer of praise. When we have asked God to do something for someone, it is then time to praise Him that He is doing it. A prayer that is filled with agony is the prayer of unbelief. If God is answering your prayer, you should be filled with joy! What if He answers your prayer in His own way rather than your way? If the police call and say your son has been picked up and is in jail for possession of dope, what will your reaction be? It all depends on whether you have really given your son to God or are holding on to him yourself. Jesus said to bring your burdens to Him and leave them there. If He has your son, you have the right to believe He is working out the best plan! Can you learn to trust in Christ instead of continually laboring over problems that only He can do anything about? Your own fear and unbelief would be the very force that ties His hands.

Of Jesus it is written, "He did not many mighty works there because of their unbelief" (Matt. 13:58).

SPEAKING IN TONGUES

Dear Rev. Carothers:

When I was prayed for to receive the baptism in the Holy Spirit, I said a few words that were not English. But I thought I made them up out of my own mind, so I wouldn't say them anymore. Now, I don't know if I received anything or not. Should I thank the Lord that I'm so mixed-up?

Dear Christian,

Yes, if you are mixed-up, you are in training to help other mixed-up people. There are quite a few of them around! Praying in a new language comes to your mind first. God has to use this part of you since this is what you are accustomed to using. When you start speaking and releasing your faith, the Spirit will take over and talk through you.

How can you be absolutely sure that the words you speak are from the Holy Spirit and not from your own imagination? One very simple way: "According to your faith be it unto you" (Matt. 9:29). Jesus spoke these words to two blind men. They knew they couldn't see, yet He encouraged them to believe they could. Jesus said a new language would be provided for everyone who would believe (Mark 16:17). Reach out your faith, claim what is yours, and it is yours. Whatever you believe is what you receive!

"He that wavereth [doubts] is like a wave of the sea driven with the wind and tossed. For let not that man think that he shall receive any thing of the Lord" (James 1:6,7).

A SHORT SEPARATION

Dear Rev. and Mrs. Carothers,

Praise the Lord! My husband gave me fifty dollars and told me to leave. I did, and shortly after, in a little church up from where I am staying, I received the baptism. They also gave me your book, *Prison to Praise*. I started thanking and praising God for my problem. In one week from the time my husband told me to leave, he came and wanted me to come back with him. Our marriage is more blessed than it ever was. I just wanted to say thank you.

My Comments

The more I see and hear, the more I know that God is able to take everything and work something glorious out of it.

"I will hope continually, and will praise thee more and more" (Ps. 71:14).

WIFE WITH CANCER

Dear Brother Carothers,

Praise the Lord! I just finished your book, *Prison to Praise*. The Holy Spirit is leading me closer and closer to our Lord every day. I praise Him for books like yours.

I was urged throughout the time I was reading the book to write to you. If, in your travels, or vacation, you ever come through Jackson Hole, Wyoming, or plan to see Yellowstone or our part of the country, please stay in our home.

In October, I found I had cancer, and I've been praising God for this. I don't understand, or rather didn't, until I read your book, why I felt praise and love for God—especially praise *for* cancer. I'm believing God for a healing. I don't know when, nor how it will come about. Now I can circulate your book among my friends and perhaps spread some understanding. Praise God! I am filled with JOY!

Since October, God has really "taken me to school," and the Holy Spirit guides me more and more as I am able to surrender "self" to Him.

My Comments

Here is a powerful example of how God can use even the dreaded disease of cancer to win men to Christ. This wife has released a powerful force as she believes God is using her infirmity to help her family. Additional letters from her have been continuously joyful and thankful.

"Don't fear anything except the Lord .... If you fear him, you need fear nothing else. He will be your safety" (Isa. 8:13,14 TLB).

DUMB OLD MAN

Dear Chaplain Carothers,

I want to thank you and God for writing such a terrific book, *Prison to Praise*. At first when I started to read it, I thought, "This is just a dumb old man who doesn't know what he's talking about." But the more I read your book, the more it made sense. By the time I was only half done, I just knew I had to write to you. When I was three-fourths done, I was almost jumping up and down for joy. What a surprise it was for me when the book gave your address. I almost jumped up and shouted, "Praise the Lord."

I was first baptized in February. At first I was really praising God, and I felt like a new person, but then it slowly faded away. Your book gave me the spiritual uplift I needed.

My Comments

So often the joy of the new Christian begins to say, "What is the reason?" Often people think, "I must not be doing enough for God, so He has taken away my joy." This is caused by the well-meaning Christians who quickly latch on to a new Christian and try to get him "organized." He is instructed in all the things he must do or not do in order to keep his new life.

If doing something didn't bring the joy in the first place, it won't keep it. The joy came in the first place when you believed that God, through Christ, gave you forgiveness of all your sins. If the joy sags, do the same thing that brought it in the first place! Consider what you may have done that hurts God. Ask His forgiveness, and then He forgives you. If your joy does not become complete, go a little deeper, and let Him reveal any weakness you may have. Believe He forgives you, and joy will flow.

Why does this work? The Holy Spirit came to the world to lift up Christ. The Holy Spirit moves when we believe Christ forgives us. The Holy Spirit always brings joy!

"When the Holy Spirit controls our lives he will produce this kind of fruit in us: love, joy, peace" (Gal. 5:22 TLB).

FROM A MOTHER WHO HAD SUFFERED MANY YEARS GRIEVING OVER THE LOSS OF HER SON

Dear Rev. Carothers,
Just a note to say thank you for your prayers. I've done like you said and given myself to Jesus and I just feel great! I go around praising the Lord for everything. Sometimes I wonder why things happen, but the Lord knows much better than I. I realize the devil was doing terrible things to me, and I was listening to him and not Jesus. No longer do I try to forget my son is gone, but I miss him so, and I miss our talks and things we did together. How wonderful it was to have him for nineteen-and-a-half years.

God has been so good to us. Before my son was taken, he sat down with my mother and talked to her about Jesus and the Bible. Mother noticed the change in him but hadn't realized he read the Bible and knew so much about it. He told Mother that he loved each of us, but he loved Jesus most of all. He also said it was very hard to be a good Christian, and he told a friend that the kids laughed at him. I just praise God for all of this. I know that he is finally at home and is happy there.

I had a dream once before my son was killed, and so did he, but we laughed about our crazy dreams and passed them off, not realizing the Lord was trying to

141

prepare us. My dream was a happy dream, although in it I left my son, but when I looked back he had a big smile, and there was a white glow around him. I have thought of these dreams so many times. I've told a few people, but they believe that it was nothing. Praise God anyway?

The direction of my life has changed, but I still have a ways to go. I do *so* want to speak in tongues—to praise the Lord. I have tried, and one lady told me she speaks in tongues and interprets also. That really discouraged me. My husband and I went to a Full Gospel meeting, and I almost ran forward to be prayed for. The speaker pulled me up front and said he would pray for me. I could hardly wait, but he proceeded to shake my head with his hands and really messed my hair up. He was so rough, I almost blurted, "Are you really a Christian?"

My husband took me out of there—fast—and will not go back to another meeting. I was so hurt by the whole thing—praise God! When I went again, I heard you. That meeting was different; I tried to get my husband to go with me the next time, but to no avail. I'm still praying that he will go again.

Dear Friend,

Probably thousands of mothers and fathers are grieving over the death of their children, not realizing that this is one of Satan's most painful tools to rob people of Jesus' peace. When Jesus said, "Let not your heart be troubled" (John 14:1), He meant He would be with us to give us peace instead of a troubled heart. If we are going to trust Him to change our decayed dead bodies into glorified bodies, we should trust Him to take away the deadness of despair over the loss of a loved one! He wants to.

As for your bad experience at the meeting you and your husband attended, sometimes well-meaning Christians try to shake, push, or pound the Holy Spirit into people, thinking their own efforts have something to do with getting someone baptized in the Spirit. Their good intentions turn many people away from an experience that should be a manifestation of the gentle shepherd who leads rather than drives his flock.

"If ye then, being evil, know how to give good gifts unto your children: how much more shall your heavenly Father give the Holy Spirit to them that ask him?" (Luke 11:13).

DOPE AND JAIL

Dear Mr. Carothers,

While here in jail, I came across your book, *Prison to Praise,* and was so interested I couldn't put it down until I finished reading it. I even plan to read it a second time. The things you said held me spellbound, and I believe every word of it.

I'm like so many men—I drink heavy, I smoke, I take drugs, I swear, my wife and I are on very shaky grounds, and I am a sinner, from A to Z. Yet through all my evil ways, I pray to God most every night, asking for forgiveness of my sins, asking Him to take away my drinking, my drug habit, and make me a different person. I have prayed with honesty, but I'm my same old self. He hasn't answered my prayer. I really and truly believe He walked this world long ago and died on the Cross for our sins, and I believe all the wonderful things He did while living as a man and that someday He'll return to this earth. I believe everything in the Bible.

Mr. Carothers, I can't come to see you and talk and pray with you, because I'm in jail. But after reading your book, I felt a strong urge to write you, and the thought came to me that if your hands were on this letter that I'm now touching, it would serve the same purpose as if your hand touched my head as we prayed to our Father in heaven. So when you get through reading this letter, will you please pray for me? For my drinking habit, and

143

drug habit, that are tearing me and my wife apart, for my smoking habit, and that I will somehow get out of this awful mess with the law that I got myself into. Pray for togetherness for myself and my wife, and ask the Lord to make me a new person. Tell Him I'm ready to do His will, and ask Him to somehow show me what He wants me to do to serve Him. Touch this letter, hold it in your hand, and pray for my forgiveness.

Pray hard that God will, at the end of this trial through the hearts of the jury, let the verdict be "Not Guilty." For sir, I did this crime under the influence of heavy drug-taking. I don't remember much about it, just short spurts. My head would try to clear, but nothing I was doing really mattered, for I was so incompetent of mind, it all seemed more of a dream. I had no control over the crime I was doing. So not only pray that I'll come out all right at the trial, but that all my sins will be taken away and that the mighty power of God will take hold of my life and make me a different person, free from drink and the craving of drugs and smoking forever. I write this letter in desperate need of your prayers.

My Comments

This is a simple, child like cry for help. I am believing that God is continuing to meet this young man's need. Will you believe with me? Can you see that while this boy was free, he could not or would not hear God's voice? And so God permitted all of the terrible vices to attack him in order to help him. You may ask, "But what about all the other men and women who are overcome by habits of one kind or another?"

God wants to use everything to help all of His creation. He has constructed this world in such a way that He gave dominion to us! Our faith and praise is the material He must use. Someone placed that book in this boy's hands. I sent the copies to the prison, but someone, like you, made it possible. God uses our acts of faith to reach out and touch those in need.

144

Dear Friend,

Jesus taught about two men who came to the Temple to pray. One man thanked God that He had never done any of the wrong things. The other man was so ashamed of his past life that he bowed his head and said that he was not worthy even to pray. He went down from the Temple with his heart made new, because God saw the honest desires of his heart. You are the second man, because you realize your great need. God hears and answers your prayers. As you hold my letter, believe that God now forgives you of all your sins and comes into your life. Believe that Christ heals you of your drinking, drugs, fear, bad habits, and everything else you want to be free of. My faith will be with yours, as you pray and believe. I have a strong understanding as I write this, that God is already reaching out to touch you, and heal you, and make you completely well. It gives me great joy to know that even at this moment, God is reaching across many miles to bring an answer to your prayer.

My Comments

I did not receive another letter from this young man, only a telephone call, saying he was out of jail and that God had indeed touched his heart, and changed his life. It had been difficult for him to realize what had happened while he was still in jail, but when he was out, he realized that he no longer had the overwhelming desire for drugs, and as his faith grew, he realized he was completely well. He couldn't express his thanks enough for what Jesus had done for him. Whatever your status in life is, your faith can reach into prisons, hospitals, the ghettos of America, or anywhere people are in need. Your ability to serve is never limited to the four walls of your hospital room, or to the confines of your home. It's free to reach out and touch all men everywhere. Christ has given you this power.

"Our greatest wish and prayer is that you will become mature Christians" (II Cor. 13:9 TLB).

MEMBERSHIP TERMINATED

Dear Rev. Carothers,

All my life I dearly loved my church. Our whole family was there, so to speak, whenever the doors opened.

Then Jesus baptized me in His Holy Spirit! I loved my church even more and eagerly shared with my pastor the beautiful thing God had done for me. He wasn't very pleased, I could tell, and said, "You must be very careful. I think you are too emotional about this thing you believe has happened to you."

I prayed for God to bless our pastor and to baptize him in the Holy Spirit so he could share with our entire congregation. I kept seeing signs that our pastor was becoming more and more irritated with me. I never said anything to anyone about my experience while I was in church, since I knew how the pastor felt, but I shared with members of the congregation when they came to our home. They responded with enthusiasm and wanted to know what had caused me to receive such joy. They said I seemed to laugh all the time, as if I had discovered something wonderful.

As I realized the need for spiritual awakening in our church, I was keenly aware that our children weren't receiving any solid teaching. Their Sunday-school classes concerned everything in the world except Jesus. I prayed for God to change our church or to lead us somewhere where my family could grow spiritually. But I knew the biggest problem God had to solve for me. My husband would never leave our church, and he definitely would not go to any church that had any kind of Pentecostal leaning. I knew God would have to perform a miracle to change our church or to get us to a place where we could all grow.

One Sunday our pastor chose to speak against the charismatic movement in the United States. He said, "Anyone who has been led into this movement is deceived by the devil. We even have one of our own members who has been deceived." He said it was all inspired and led by the devil. At this point he did something that has never been known to happen in the history of our church. He said, "I now remove Mrs. (he called my name) from the membership of this church. She is no longer a member, and I invite her to leave." I was so shocked I couldn't have moved if the church had been on fire.

When we got home, my husband was more angry than I have ever seen him. He said, "I'll never go back to that church again, and none of my family will ever go again. You pick out whatever church you want, and we will go there."

As my brain cleared, I saw that God had worked His miracle! I picked out a church where we are now hearing the blessed Gospel of faith in Jesus, and where the pastor and people believe in being baptized in the Holy Spirit. To my joyful surprise, my husband seems right at home. He still has not shown an interest in being baptized himself, but he is perfectly willing for the children and me to pray as we want to. What a wonderful God we have! How glad I am that you taught me to praise Him. From the very beginning, I thanked God for my pastor as he was and I still do.

My Comments

Yes, in everything give thanks. God is perfectly capable of working everything out if we trust Him. Miracles are His business! He uses our faith as the material He works with.

"Blessed be the name of God for ever and ever: for wisdom and might are his" (Dan. 2:20).

"To the only wise God our Savior, be glory and majesty, dominion and power, both now and ever. Amen" (Jude 25).

DEATH

Dear Sir,

When I hear of all the terrible men who are in the world and how ugly and mean they treat their wives and families, I cannot understand why I should thank God for my husband's death. He was the kindest, most loving man that God ever made. We very seldom had any harsh words for each other, and our house was a place of love. He worked hard, provided for his family, and loved to be at home with us. He led us in our family prayers and was in every way the head of our home. And yet, while he was still very young, God permitted him to die. I am unable to be at peace, and I ask for your prayers and help.

My Comments

I would never profess to know why sorrows come into our lives or why there are often so many tears. I do know that God is God and that He is watching over every one of us. I do not know why we must part from our loved ones; I only know that God has promised us eternal life. I know that regardless of whatever comes into our lives, we must believe. No matter what any day may bring, God has promised it will be for the best.

When my own father died, I was twelve years old. My next younger brother was seven, and the baby brother was only one year old. My father was only thirty-six. He had never been sick a day in his life. He was looked up to by the community as the best Christian man they had ever known. He was loved and respected by everyone who knew him. He was just a laborer in a factory, but he made his mark on the community by his love for Christ. When he walked down the aisles of the United States Steel Mill in Elwood City, Pennsylvania, he would shout out to the men as he passed them, "Praise the Lord." His loving, joyful smile captivated everyone who knew him. He loved people and they loved him. He used every spare minute of his life in doing something for others.

After he died, I'm sure that many people asked the question, "Why did God let Dave Carothers die?" Perhaps many people were unable to thank and to praise God and could not understand how anything good could possibly come from the death of such an unusual man.

Years after his death, when I went back to work in the same factory, very old men would come to the little office where I was working and with hat in hand would try to tell me what they remembered about my father. I can still remember the tears that came into their eyes as they expressed what they felt. Their words were like this: "Son, if you can grow up to be half the man your father was, you will be a great man." I heard these words many times and often wondered, "Why did God take my father when we needed him so much?"

Now I know and understand that God had a much higher purpose and plan than I could see. He used my father's life and death for His own purpose. God used my sorrow to teach me to trust and praise Him. God has supplied all my needs, exceedingly abundantly, above all that I could ask or hope for. He has supplied the needs of my mother and my two brothers again and again. God has made it very clear to me that even though other people did not understand, He had His own plan. Now I thank Him and praise Him for doing what He knew was good.

"The Lord is righteous in all his ways, and holy in all his works" (Ps. 145:17).

MARRIAGE TO BOY FROM CHICAGO

A country girl married a boy from a wealthy Chicago family. She was immediately immersed in rounds of parties and a pace completely foreign to her. Her husband, to her horror, was, along with other members of his family, smoking pot. She gritted her teeth and did her best to stick by her marriage vows, but the nightly rounds of drinking, pot parties, and wild LSD trips by her husband and his friends caused her such mental anguish that she considered leaving. It was all like an impossible nightmare. He laughed and scorned her insistence that this life was all wrong. When she finally told her husband she was leaving, he agreed to give up the drug route.

Soon after this the husband was drafted and in time was sent to Vietnam. There he renewed his drug use and moved on to even harder drugs. His letters boasted of the parties and wild living. The young wife lived in continual frustration. Should she go back to living with this wild young man when he returned, or make this the final break with his way of living? Each day she changed her mind and could think of little else. Then came a calm determination. She would not let herself be pulled into the hopeless pit of drugs. She didn't believe in divorce, but wrote her husband and told him she could never again live with him and asked him not to see her when he returned from Vietnam. She knew his reaction would be, "Do whatever you want to do."

Then a friend loaned her a copy of *Prison to Praise*. There she learned about being thankful to God. Immediately she applied it to her own life and found faith to believe that God would solve the entire situation. Her fears, frustrations, and husband, she gave over to God and thanked Him for everything exactly as it was.

In two weeks an amazing letter reached her from Vietnam. Her husband had changed his entire way of living! He had completely given up dope and had gone to the chaplain requesting advice on how to live a Christian life. The wife exclaimed, "I had begged, pleaded, and threatened my husband, and nothing had helped. I praised God, and see what He did!"

When the young man came home, he and his wife went on to build a Christian home and family.

"Blessed be the Lord, who daily loadeth us with benefits, even the God of our salvation" (Ps. 68:19).

DOPE CHARGE DROPPED

One of the most frequent and shattering problems facing modern parents is for a child to be picked up on a dope charge. When one son was arrested for possession of marijuana and other illegal drugs, the parents immediately responded in praise and thanksgiving. They have been believing for God to work a miracle in their son's life, and they accepted this as part of God's work. The boy had been picked up in a state park, while in their automobile, and there was the possibility of their losing their car as well as the probability of their son's imprisonment.

As the time for the hearing neared, the parents increased their praise for the entire incident. Their attorney tried to make them more aware of the gravity of the situation by warning them that recent cases of this same nature had resulted in the imprisonment of the offenders. The community was aroused over crimes being committed by young people trying to get money for more drugs, and the prosecuting attorney was having to press for convictions. The mother and father increased their thanksgiving. Even the son was amazed that his parents were not "all steamed up," as they used to get over much more minor incidents.

At the hearing, everyone connected with the case was astounded. The judge listened to all the evidence and pronounced the son guilty of being on state property at an unauthorized time and fined him five dollars. No one connected with the case could make any sense out of the verdict! Those who walk in the Spirit grow to expect the unusual.

———————

"Now unto him that is able to do exceeding abundantly above all that we ask or think, according to the power that worketh in us" (Eph. 3:20).

"Most gladly therefore will I rather glory in my infirmities, that the power of Christ may rest upon me" (II Cor. 12:9).

LUNGS HEALED IN OHIO

Dear Sir,

I shall always remember you as Colonel Carothers and sincerely thank and praise God for sending you to our town. I was a very ill person, both mentally and physically, when you prayed, and God healed me. I have taken no nerve medication or visited a doctor since last January (except for chest X rays). Just a few months before you came to Marion, I was told by my physician that I would need lung surgery. Since X rays (and all kinds of tests) showed lesions on the left lower lobe, numerous ones were taken, the kind that takes pictures of every layer of lung tissue.

For some reason, I pleaded for more time. Although I became very despondent, feeling sorry for myself and very

152

bitter, I knew this was wrong. All the doctors did for me was load me with pills and various nerve medicines.

Being a nurse for forty years, I realized what was in store for me, and in my weakness, Satan went to work. I became so despondent that I was thinking of an easy way out. (God forgive me.) Self-pity took over. I had been a bedside nurse for forty years, and a Christian even longer than that. And I did not think it fair for me to have to suffer with no one to care for me—I thought.

Somehow, I found strength enough to get ready for the service that morning. I said to my husband, "Don't ask any questions about why I am so determined to go." He came along, thinking that he would have to take me to the emergency room at any time.

Colonel Carothers, when you prayed, God healed me. I have since had three chest X-rays, and they are okay. My lungs are clear. After the first X-ray in February, the doctor called me and said, "I have good news for you."

I said, "Yes, I know what it is." I think he thought I was out of my mind. However, he said, "The lesions have cleared." I was overjoyed and said thanks and praised God for healing me. Two more chest X-rays since then have been negative.

I've never felt better or happier. All the burden was lifted. I have not been depressed and have more interest in life than ever before. I get tired at times, I mean physically, because I take care of my patient and help the girls with twenty-five others on this wing.

I have read *Prison to Praise* many times and received great blessings. I have loaned it to others, and the reorders, I gave to special friends.

If you are ever near our town, like within a radius of a hundred miles, please let us know so we'll have the opportunity of hearing you again.

Many people have heard my testimony. The doctors look at me in wonder when they see how healthy and happy I am and how hard I work. It seems that I cannot praise God enough for what He has done for me.

My Comments

Most Christians would be willing to endure a physical infirmity if they knew that God was going to heal them. I am often asked how we can pray for God to heal us, if we are thankful that we are ill. My answer to this is, that we could never be healed unless we were first sick. Therefore, when God permits Satan to attack our physical bodies, we can believe that God wanted to use this for some glorious purpose. We can then thank Him and believe that He knew what would help us. We can also thank Him that He has given us the desire to be well. There are many unfortunate people who do not even desire to be well. Since we want to be well, we can pray, "God, I thank You for my desire to be well, and I ask You, in Jesus' name, to heal me." It is then our opportunity to praise Him and to thank Him for our healing.

Do not be disturbed if the symptoms remain. That is God's problem. Our responsibility is to thank Him that He is healing us. How long should it take? That also is not our problem. God does not look at time as we do. He is only interested in what is best for you and for me. If it should take physical infirmity to build our faith and trust in Him, this is what He will permit to happen. The natural, human reaction is to think that perfect health would be more likely to build our faith than sickness. But everyday experiences prove this not to be true.

When we are well in body, our faith is usually not stimulated to believe. Faith grows when results are not apparent. Therefore, faith is not dependent upon what we can see. It is dependent on what we believe. If God gives you the gift of having some need, and gives you the desire to pray for that need, rejoice if He permits your faith to continually reach out to trust Him, regardless of the circumstances. So many people lose heart when they do not see results. They are unaware that lack of results is often God's gift to help us learn to trust Him.

You may say, "Merlin Carothers is trying to sidestep

the issue," but I am sharing with you the wonderful power there is when we learn to trust God for what He is rather than for what He does.

———————

"He that spared not his own Son, but delivered him up for all, how shall he not with him also freely give us all things?" (Rom. 8:32).

PRISON WARDEN

Dear Chaplain Carothers,

Several elderly ladies came into our prison to leave books for the prisoners to read. My job as warden requires me to be polite, but I confess I was very scornful of their efforts to change the men. I knew that no book was going to change any of our men, and I didn't believe in any extra effort to entertain them.

When the ladies were gone, I glanced through the books to see what they were distributing. Most of them looked harmless enough, but my eye caught one title, *Prison to Praise*. Since there were several of them, I kept one, and for lack of anything better to do, decided to read it. A guard took the rest back to the cells. For the rest of the evening, I read your book. It intrigued me, to say the least, but left me skeptical.

The next day the prison chaplain came by and asked if I had ever read a book called *Prison to Praise*. I was a little embarrassed to have to say, "Yes, why?"

"One of the men read it last night, and it seems to have caused a great change in his life."

When he told me the man's name, I said, "That won't last long with him."

The chaplain said, "I know what you mean, but this seems to be genuine."

In the following days, I went out of my way several

times to either see or check up on the man the chaplain had told me about. Every time he came to my attention, it had something to do with his praising God. He praised God for anything and everything. Prior to this, he had been surly, bitter, and always ready to fight anyone about anything. His new attitude was amazing. It was also contagious. Other men followed his example. Everywhere I turned, the atmosphere was different than it had ever been. Gradually my natural skepticism gave way, and I became a believer. I accepted Christ myself, and I now know Him as you write about Him. If you have any other good books I can share with the prisoners, please let me know.

———————

"When saw we thee sick, or in prison, and came unto thee? ... As ye have done it unto one of the least of these my brethren, ye have done it unto me" (Matt. 25:39,40).

A DESERTER TO SWEDEN

Dear Brother Carothers,
You don't know who I am, but that doesn't make any difference. We are both children of God, and that is all that matters. At this moment I am sitting in a cell of a stockade located at Fort Riley. The reason I am in prison is because I deserted my unit in Germany and put myself in exile in Sweden for two-and-a-half years. This is the first time I have been home in four-and-a-half years.

The reason I am writing to you is that I have just finished reading your book, *Prison to Praise*. I just wanted to tell you how much I enjoyed it and how much it helped to strengthen my faith. I can truly see that God has shown His infinite wisdom through you and that you have used Christ in the way He wants to be used. Of course, there is no other way Christ can be used effectively.

My own testimony for Christ began six years ago when I was seventeen. My mother and father had just recently been converted and filled with the baptism in the Holy Spirit. I saw how God was working a miracle in their lives, so I accepted Jesus as my personal Savior and grew in Christ for one year, then started to slide back into my old ways again. Shortly after this, I went into the Army, and then I got turned on with drugs. This started four-and-a-half long years of sorrow for me and my family.

Soon after turning on, I became a typical flower-child with typical flower-child ideas and conceptions. I decided the Army was wrong, and in order to make my newfound freedom known to the brass, I split to Sweden. Once in Sweden, it was more drugs and faster living. But you know what? God was there all the time, gently pulling me home. It took four-and-a-half years for me to finally say, "Okay, Lord, I am Yours. Do with me as You see fit."

I have never been so happy before in my life. God has revealed great things to me just in the week since I have returned home. I am awaiting a whole lifetime of being in Jesus and Jesus in me. Praise God! Isn't it truly wonderful how Jesus loves us? I dedicate my whole life to Him and praise His wonderful name. Christ has taught me through you to trust Him completely. I have no fear in me now. I know I am safe. Praise God.

Brother Carothers, I am truly grateful for your book and would very much like to meet you personally. If we don't meet in this life, then I will see you in heaven.

My Comments

When young Christians stray away from God, parents have every right to believe that God will draw them back to Himself. Our faith in Him releases His power to draw His children to Himself. As He uses us to win men to Christ, He uses our faith to draw them back. Literally

157

thousands of young people have returned to Jesus after reading *Prison to Praise*. They see that He is really alive, and this quickens their faith.

"Teach a child to choose the right path, and when he is older he will remain upon it" (Prov. 22:6 TLB).

HANDS OFF STEERING WHEEL

"The car was speeding down the highway. My hands moved farther and farther from the steering wheel. This was impossible. It couldn't be happening! I must be dreaming. The harder I tried to get hold of the steering wheel, the farther my hands moved away from it. An irresistible power was forcing my hands toward the sides of the automobile. I had never felt the power of God before, Dad; in fact, I didn't believe such a power existed."

These words poured from a teen-age boy as he recounted to his father his experiences of two hours before.

It really had started a long time ago, when Tom had decided he no longer wanted to have anything to do with his father's and mother's religion. God and Jesus and the Holy Spirit were for people who didn't have anything better to do with their time. He had a lifetime of excitement ahead of him and didn't want to be saddled with the extra burden of trying to be "religious."

Tom's parents prayed fervently for him, but nothing seemed to happen. They tried restricting their son when he became too belligerent, taking away privileges. They tried more prayer, more generous portions of kindness and love, but nothing did any observable good. Tom became more and more enamored of staying out late at night, drinking, using foul language, and finally became involved with drugs. When his parents realized this, a deathly fear gripped their hearts. The son they loved so much appeared to be throwing his life away, and they felt helpless. To make matters worse, Tom's father was a Baptist preacher. All of this made it look to others as if there must be something sinister wrong "in the preacher's house."

I first met Tom's father one evening at the close of a meeting where I had just spoken. His face was radiant. He glowed with a joy that caused me to think, "There's a man who knows the real joy there is in Jesus." He came up to me half-laughing and half-saying, "Praise the Lord." He was really alive!

He said, "I'm a Baptist minister who has been filled with the Holy Spirit. It happened only two weeks ago, and I haven't touched the ground yet." I could see that he was still intoxicated with the joy of the Spirit of Jesus.

He then told me what had happened a few days after he received the baptism. He had a telephone call from Tom's school, asking him to come and talk with the principal. He went and received new evidence of his son's great need for help. "Why hasn't Tom been coming to school?" the principal asked.

"I thought he was!" Tom's father protested. "He has been leaving home every morning at school time."

"No, he hasn't been attending classes," the principal explained. "I've just learned that he has been going up into the mountains to a cabin with other boys and spending the day drinking and smoking pot. You are going to have to do something with him."

On the way home, the father felt discouragement beginning to drain off the new joy he had just recently received. He then remembered something he had read in a book called *Prison to Praise*. He had read about the power in thanking God for all things and believing that God would work out everything for good if we trusted Him. So, all the way home he praised God for this new experience with Tom and believed that God was blessing Tom even though he as a father couldn't see it.

When he arrived home, he took Tom into the study and told him, "I've just been talking to the principal and he has told me what you have been doing."

At first Tom looked surprised, but then a mask of sullenness came over his face. He was ready for one more argument and one more lecture about how much he needed to let God have his life. To his surprise, and even to his father's surprise, he heard these words:

"Tom, I've learned something new that you wouldn't understand yet, but I'm turning you over to God. I'm going to trust Him now to do whatever is best in your life. I have done the best I know how to do, and it hasn't worked, so I'm going to let God do to you whatever He wants to do. I have a great peace about you now, and I'm actually thankful for your life exactly as it is."

"The old man has really flipped his lid now," the boy thought.

The father then had to leave to attend a meeting at his church. He was still flooded with joy. Christ was literally bearing all his burdens for him. When he returned two-and-a-half hours later, Tom was sitting on the couch, laughing and crying at the same time. He sat down beside him and asked, "What's wrong, Tom?"

"When you left, I went out to the car and decided to look up some of my friends for some excitement. As I was driving down the road, a powerful force pulled my hands off the steering wheel."

The father's first thought was, "He's wrecked the car!" But then he realized he had seen the car out front when he came in.

"When I was terrified for fear the car was going to wreck, I heard a voice. It said, 'Turn off the road and stop.'

"I heard the voice, but couldn't tell where it was coming from. I tried again to reach the steering wheel so I could pull off the road. This time, my hands easily reached the wheel, and I pulled over and stopped.

" 'Your father gave you to me.'

"The voice spoke to me again, and I knew it was God.

But then I thought 'It couldn't be God. He doesn't even exist.'

" 'Now you will repent and ask for My forgiveness?' the voice said.

"I suddenly realized what a sinner I was. I could feel and see and understand all at the same time how miserable a person I had become. I started to cry and kept asking God to forgive me. When I had asked for forgiveness for everything I could think of, I felt a kind of joy filling me up inside. I laughed and cried at the same time. I haven't been able to stop since."

As the father told me this story, he had to stop occasionally to say, "Praise the Lord." God had done something for him because he had believed God. His joy was full and overflowing.

"For if you give, you will get! Your gift will return to you in full and overflowing measure, pressed down, shaken together to make room for more, and running over. Whatever measure you use to give—large or small—will be used to measure what is given back to you" (Luke 6:38).

DAY BEFORE CHRISTMAS

Dear Chaplain Carothers,

The day before Christmas, my husband left me and our three children. He left us no food, no presents, no money, and nowhere to go. He said he would never be coming back, and I have not seen him since.

Perhaps you can imagine the absolute terror that I felt. The only solution that I could think of was for a sudden end to my own life and that of my children. When neighbors heard what had happened, they came to offer their help. They weren't able to do very much for me,

161

since they didn't have much themselves, but they gave me a copy of your book, *Prison to Praise*. As I read it, the fear drained out of me. I knew that Christ was there with me. I have been a Christian for a long while, but I never knew that God could help me so much when I had problems.

Even though I am still alone with my children, I have a feeling I never had before. It's like, "Wow, God really *does* love me. Even if no one else in all the world loves me, He does." I know that He is working out my life and my children's. I know there isn't much I could do but trust Him, but as I trust Him, I'm having so much fun.

My husband didn't want me teaching the children about Jesus. But now I am free to teach them at any time. We have so much fun singing and laughing and talking about Jesus.

Thank you for writing your book.

My Comments

At times a parent may be more detrimental to children than good. It is not at all difficult to see that God loves children so much that He often permits things to happen for their benefit. They may not understand this at the time, but in years to come or in eternity each one will understand why God permitted all things in their lives.

"O Lord, I will honor and praise your name, for you are my God; you do such wonderful things" (Isa. 25:1 TLB).

GUARD SAVED

Dear Brother Carothers,

Greetings in our Lord's wonderful name. I thought I would write and let you know some of the good news that is happening in this prison since I was baptized in the Holy Spirit as a result of reading your *Prison to Praise* The Spirit is really moving among the men here at the prison. There have been some thirteen men saved since the first of the year, plus one guard. There have been five of these men who have received the baptism in the Holy Spirit with the evidence of speaking in tongues.

I will tell you what happened just two or three weeks ago when a guard found the Lord. We (five of the inmates here at the prison) were coming back from a prayer meeting where three of the men received the baptism in the Holy Spirit. We all went to another inmate's cell. However, only one inmate is allowed to a cell at this time, so we knew that the guards would chase us out shortly, but we wanted to have some fellowship and prayer together.

A minute after we got to the cell, a guard did come to chase us out. We all shouted, "Praise the Lord!" and asked him to come in to pray with us. All that happened was that the guard opened his mouth like a fish that was drowning but said nothing. He turned around, and at a very fast rate (almost a run), left the cell. We started to pray, and while we were praying, another guard came to chase us out but said nothing either. He also left.

Still a different guard came to chase us out, and this time we were through praying. He came to the cell door and couldn't say anything either (by his own testimony later). We said, "Praise the Lord," and the two men who had just been baptized started to witness to this guard. As they told him what the Lord had done for them and what He meant to them, the guard slowly slid down the wall and sat on the floor, half in the cell and half out of the cell, crying. I asked him if he would like us to pray for him, and he said yes. I asked Joe to pray for him. Without at first knowing what to say, he asked the guard to repeat after him the sinner's prayer of repentance and acceptance of Christ. This the guard did, and he was saved while sitting on the cell floor.

I won't go into some of the miracles that have been happening in my life since I have completely turned my life over to Christ, but there have been many. There are many men who have found the Lord, and their lives have changed and are continuing to change. I have contacted some bookstores, and they have sent some books, so I have started a Christian lending library here at the prison. I try to be led by the Spirit as to what books to loan to each man. I would like to know if you could send me any more copies of your *Prison to Praise*. We have used up all that we had and could use more. This book has really been a blessing to many men in here.

Would you also have at least one copy of *Power in Praise?* Also would you have any other books that you could send us that could be used in our library here? The Lord bless you, and I trust you are having a blessed time in the Lord.

My Comments

Similar letters from all over the United States have compelled me to form the corporation, Foundation of Praise, Inc. Through this means, I hope to get copies of *Prison to Praise* and other books into the hands of thousands of prisoners, hospital patients, and into the most needy hands in the world. This book is now printed in Spanish, and some are working to have it translated in several other languages as well. You can support the Foundation of Praise whenever you desire.

"The jailer fell down before Paul and Silas. He ... begged them, "Sirs, what must I do to be saved?" (Acts 16:29 TLB).

PRAISE GOD FOR PNEUMONIA

Dear Mr. Carothers,

Enclosed is an order. May I have another order blank? I've given away at least fifty copies of *Prison to Praise*

The principle has most assuredly been meaningful in my life. I left Corpus Christi on February 23 to keep two of my grandchildren while their mother went to the Orient on a buying trip. I had been coughing since October, but the doctor said it was just an allergy, so I went on about my business with great effort since I felt so bad. While I was with my grandchildren, I got pneumonia and was so sick. I just kept thanking God for the pneumonia and telling Him that I didn't understand it, but I knew He did. I got back home on Palm Sunday eve, still feeling spent and sick. The doctor put me in the hospital for the breathing machine, to which I responded. There had been X-rays and nothing showed, but a new X-ray showed trouble.

To make a long story short, I had surgery for lung cancer. The doctor removed the middle lobe of my right lung—which had dried up with a self-contained cancer. He got it all, and I'm recuperating now.

Now I see the greatness of pneumonia, for it made me pursue the illness. I'm so glad I could thank God through it all. My whole recovery has surprised the doctors. They can't understand why I have recovered so rapidly, but I know it was praise! While I was so ill with pneumonia, I could not seem to pray, but I could always praise. I learned from Rom. 8:26-28 that I don't have to pray, since the Holy Spirit will take control. Also I'm claiming v. 28 and know that all this is working for my good since I do love the Lord and am trying to do His will and fit into His purpose.

As soon as I am able, I am going to pursue the possibility of your coming to our town Already three have said they will help to underwrite the cost. Praise the Lord! Thank you for your witness.

I gave my doctor a copy of both of your books. The next day he came in my room and saw a copy of your new book on the chair. He asked me if I was planting them, to which I replied, "Everywhere I can!" I thank God for your ministry.

My Comments

Dear God, I thank You that You are, even when men think You are not. You are kind when men believe You to be unconcerned. You weep at the pain of men when we think You don't even care. You are alive and moving and working in our lives even when we think we are all alone.

I thank You that You love every man enough to actually reveal Yourself to anyone who seeks You. But Father, there are people reading this prayer who have never seen You or anything that they understood to be You. Please open their hearts so they will know You as You are. Let them feel Your love for them. Let them come to know someone who will demonstrate Your love to them.

Let us in every breath we breathe know that You are God and so live that others will want to know and love You.

"The Lord reigneth; let the earth rejoice" (Ps. 97:1).

PATHWAYS TO ANSWERS

It is the nature of man to work. He works to achieve, to build security, to impress others. He works even harder to find ways to get out of work. God cuts sharply into the grain of natural man and says men's works will never lead to Him. Our works are egotistical, self-centered at their very best. God's works are holy and were perfectly manifested in Christ.

Jesus urged us to let go of our paltry visions of self-achievement. Yet, He is continually confronted with our highest opinions of our own worth. He gave Peter eternal life as a free gift. Peter knew this and appreciated it. Yet Peter said he was willing to die for Christ. He was not, yet thought he was.

What good do you think you are doing? Peter said he would never deny Jesus. What evil do you think you would never do? Jesus knew that Peter was human and therefore capable of falling. He knows that you are human and capable of falling. There is no sin that you are incapable of committing. At this point I know that I am "where angels fear to tread," for you may be very positive that there are some things you would never ever do. Since you are convinced that you would never do them, you may feel justified in heaping all kinds of criticism upon others who are guilty. I believe that in order to appreciate God's great love for us, we must realize that anything in our life that resembles good is the result of God's careful protection of us over all influences that are being brought to bear upon us.

General Wright, U. S. Army, tells of the unbelievable animal characteristics that raised their ugly heads when Christian young men were involved in the Bataan death march. When confined in the hold of the ship with no fresh air, no sunlight, no food, and no water, and 100 degree heat for many days, the men seemingly lost most of their resemblance to civilized man. When one of their number was hit by a bullet from an American plane that was strafing the ship, they literally sucked the blood from the body of the dying man!

Insane? Yes, they were. But that same insanity lurks within you. You may not want to admit it, so you pull your robes of righteousness close about you and declare your complete allegiance to everything good and holy. God sees you a little differently and declares that in you "dwelleth no good thing." Does it hurt too much to admit this? The more you admit it, the more quickly you

167

can permit Christ's righteousness to be yours. You can freely admit that the capacity to deny Christ, swear you never knew Him, steal bread for your dying children, etc., lurk within you, but that your hope is not in you, your trust is in Christ! You confess that you are no better than other men. You cannot condemn their failures, for you know that their failures lurk within you and could come into full bloom, given the right opportunity. But you also rejoice in faith that Christ has become your eternal life, and that your newborn spirit will one day leave this decrepit flesh and rise to a new world of holiness in Him (Rom. 8:10).

God could keep you holy in word, thought, and deed, but it would have to be Him doing it. Paul declared that trying to obtain salvation by our own works brought God's anger (Rom. 4:15). This most of us can't understand. But he further declares that even trying to obtain God's blessings by keeping His laws causes Him to be angry! This is hard for the natural man to understand. The whole picture points to God's absolute insistence that we come to Him trusting only in Christ, as Paul said, "The more we trust Him, the more clearly we see."

Since you have been saved from your sins through trusting Christ, how much less guilty of sin are you than the "unsaved"? Consider a scale from number one to ten, with number ten being the unsaved and "breaking all ten commandments," and Jesus being zero or "breaking none." Where do you fall in this scale? Please give this an honest effort. Decide. Where do you think you fall on the scale? If you average up your failures, do. you hit about number four or five? If so, you have somewhat to boast in, for at least you are not failing as much as a number ten man. You can take him aside and say, "Friend, I too used to be a number ten man, but then Christ saved me, and I became a number four man. You too, could be better if you would let Him do this for you!"

Sound logical? It does to me, but according to Christ it is no He said if you are a number one man you are also a number ten man and guilty of breaking all of

God's laws. If you are willing to be classified as a number ten man by God, your friends, your church, your community, you are then free to believe that God through Christ has forgiven you of all your sins and given you eternal life. Now, with great peace you can look at yourself as you are, as you could be, as you might be, and know that there is nothing within you, around you, or any part of you that God does not forgive through Christ. You are then free to look at your fellowmen as they are, for you know that whatever evil they do, it is nothing that you are incapable of, and that any goodness that others see in you is merely a demonstration of what God has done for you. What a blessed day it will be when God's children no longer condemn one another, when they feel a sense of complete dependence upon what Christ has done and is doing for them. This opens the heart to the real spirit of praise. We are then on a pathway that leads to answers to praise.

Publishers note:

Comments, inquiries, and requests for speaking engagements should be directed to:

Merlin Carothers
Box 2085
Escondido, CA 92025

ANSWERS TO PRAISE

Other Books By Merlin Carothers
Over 6 million copies sold worldwide

Praise Works (P060-4) Astounding testimonies to the power of praise from people in every walk of life. Includes questions from readers of praise books.

Power in Praise (L342-6) This second book by Merlin Carothers teaches the secret of freedom and joy through praise.

Prison to Praise (P367-3) Immensely popular bestseller has taught countless Christians the way to change their destiny through praise. Carothers writes compellingly on praising the Lord in all situations.

Victory on Praise Mountain (P410-1) How does a preacher praise God when everything he values is threatened? Merlin Carothers gives a dramatic account of his struggle to practice what he preaches.

Walking and Leaping (P104-0) Merlin Carothers shares the effects in his own life of living out the principles of praising God which he developed in *Prison to Praise* and *Power in Praise*.

Listen to Merlin Carothers Teach
On 2 Series of Tapes

Prison to Praise   6 cassettes
Power in Praise   6 cassettes

Both packaged in attractive, convenient albums.
Merlin Carothers' books and tapes available in Christian bookstores or write for information and catalog to:

Logos International
201 Church Street
Plainfield, NJ 07060

Other bestselling books
on praise from Logos:

Let Us Praise By Judson Cornwall (P039-8) Prominent charismatic leader provides "how-to" guidance on praising God. Here is a spiritual manual of life in the Spirit.

Thanks Lord, I Needed That! By Charlene Potterbaum (P248-5) Author of *This is Really for the Birds*, Charlene Potterbaum presents a human look at praising God in day-to-day situations.

Read The Magazine Reporting
Worldwide Spiritual Renewal

Logos Journal sold in many Christian bookstores

Write for information to:
Logos Journal
201 Church Steet
Plainfield, NJ 07060